BY THE AUTHOR OF

PEOPLE WHO MAKE THINGS:
How American Craftsmen Live and Work

(A MARGARET K. MC ELDERRY BOOK)

AMISH PEOPLE

MICHAEL RAMSEY

CAROLYN MEYER

AMISH PEOPLE

Plain Living In A Complex World

Photographs by Michael Ramsey,
Gerald Dodds and Carolyn Meyer

A Margaret K. McElderry Book

ATHENEUM 1976 NEW YORK

974.8

M

The author wishes to thank the Lancaster
Mennonite Conference Historical Society.

LIBRARY OF CONGRESS CATALOGING IN PUBLICATION DATA

Meyer, Carolyn.   Amish people.
"A Margaret K. McElderry book."
Summary: Describes the way of life of an Amish
family in Lancaster County, Pennsylvania,
including their work, beliefs, and customs.
1. Amish—Juvenile literature. [1. Amish.
2. Family life] I. Title.
BX8129.A6M45   974.8'15   75-28272
ISBN 0-689-50041-6

Published simultaneously in Canada by
McClelland & Stewart, Ltd.
Manufactured in the United States of America
by The Murray Printing Company
Forge Village, Massachusetts
Designed by Suzanne Haldane
First Edition

Contents

AMISH PEOPLE

FAMILY

Samuel Beiler
and His Kin

S AMUEL BEILER would give a lot to own a car.

Sam is seventeen. He works from dawn until dark on his father's farm. And he knows exactly what kind of a car he wants: a metallic blue two-door hardtop with cream-colored upholstery, black racing stripes, wide, slick tires, and a tape deck. He thinks about that car when he is plowing the tobacco fields, when he's cleaning the barn, when he's sitting through the long Sunday morning preaching, and especially when he's visiting his cousin Ben, who has hidden such a car behind a service station a few miles from his home so his parents won't find out.

Samuel Beiler and his cousin Ben are Amish, and ac-cording to the *Ordnung*—the rules of the church that govern every detail of Amish life—cars are not allowed. Sam knows that his father would throw him off the farm. His mother would never stop crying. His sisters would refuse to speak to him. His older brother would shake his head and turn away. Amos and Elam, the younger boys, would look at him with a mixture of admiration and disapproval.

Ben suspects that *his* father suspects what is going on, but since Ben is not yet baptized, he is not subject to the *Ordnung*. His father, if he knows, may be letting him get the "wildness" out of his system before he settles down. But Samuel's father is a stricter parent.

Sometimes Sam meets Ben and goes out with him and his friends. They ride up to New Holland with the radio blaring, and the one among them who looks oldest stops off to buy beer, which is also taboo. Sam is aching to drive Ben's car, but so far he hasn't been offered the chance. He can do without electricity, which is prohibited by the *Ordnung;* he sees not much point in it unless he could plug in a television set, which is also forbidden. He doesn't feel the pressing urge to have a tractor that so many of the young men—and some of the older ones—do. The *Ordnung* prohibits tractors, but he likes his team, and they work well for him. A horse and buggy has its place, but it's no substitute for a car.

Unless Samuel leaves the Amish church to which he belongs and joins a less conservative church with a more liberal *Ordnung*, he'll probably never have a car. There is the chance, a remote possibility, that the church fathers will relent, but there is very little change among the

Amish, and what change there is is accomplished with agonizing slowness. Samuel may have a gray beard before cars are permitted in his particular church.

Sometimes Sam thinks about leaving the church. There are always stories about those who have. There are also stories about those who leave and come back, unable to adapt to "the world." What would he do if he left? Work in a factory somewhere? Be shunned by his family for the rest of his life?

That is the problem. The ultimate control exerted by the Amish to keep the members in strict adherence to the *Ordnung* is the *Meidung:* shunning. No one will speak to the person or eat with him or conduct business with him or have anything whatever to do with him while he is under the ban. It can last for a lifetime, unless the sinner mends his ways, begs for forgiveness, and is re-admitted to fellowship by a unanimous vote of the congregation. It is terrible. Sam knows some it has happened to. He doesn't think he could survive it.

And besides, he loves farming. He will have to do without the car.

The four lanes of Pennsylvania Route 30 cut east from York, cross the Susquehanna River south of Harrisburg, and take a northern loop around Lancaster. To that point Route 30 is a divided highway with fast-moving traffic, but on the eastern end of Lancaster it narrows and slows down, carrying tourists to Pennsylvania Dutch country, past shopping centers with such unlikely attractions as the "Amish Cinema," past souvenir shops that sell "Amish stuff," and restaurants featuring countless dishes of "authentic Pennsylvania Dutch food," between the pizza huts and hamburger joints and the tourist attractions that purport to show "how the Amish really live." The road deposits visitors at elaborate resort motels decorated with hex signs and silhouettes of Amish buggies.

This section of Route 30 is an ugly and commercialized strip, developed in response to the "outside world's" natural curiosity about the Amish, the "plain people," whose simple, hard-working, exemplary lives are founded on abhorrence and avoidance of just such crass commercialism. Those who stay on Route 30 pass eventually, according to the map, through Paradise.

Determined tourists detour by way of Route 340 that splits off from Route 30 just east of Lancaster and passes through Smoketown, Bird-in-Hand, Intercourse (the name never fails to titillate the visitors), and White Horse. Traffic on Route 340, a narrow blacktop never designed to handle the plague of automobiles that descends upon it in the summer season, is often slowed by the horse-drawn buggies of the Amish. Drivers wait with varying degrees of patience for a chance to pass, and often there is a glimpse of a telephoto lens on a camera loaded with high-speed film, as a determined photographer attempts to "steal" a photograph of the bearded patriarch in the broad-brimmed hat who holds the reins. But the Amish driver is on guard; he turns his head away sharply.

There are tourist attractions along Route 340, but fewer of them. This is not yet a "strip," but it's going that way. In between the "Amish" motels, the "Amish" res-

A young man in his bachelor buggy drives his sisters through highway traffic. MICHAEL RAMSEY

taurants, the "Amish" gift shops, and the "Amish" school house—none of which is Amish at all—are the real Amish farms. No electric wires lead into the neat, well-kept buildings from the power lines along the road; their absence is one feature that distinguishes Amish farms from their non-Amish neighbors. The farms are rather small— no more than fifty or sixty acres, all that can be handled by a farmer limited to horse-power. Tractors, like electricity, are taboo among most of the Amish.

Tourism in Lancaster County continues to grow as more and more people, fatigued by and disenchanted with the pressures of urbanized, mechanized, high-pressure society, romanticize about the "simple life" and head for Lancaster County to take a look from an air-conditioned automobile or the tinted window of a tour bus at a folk society that is still much like it was two hundred years ago. They eat shoofly pie that resembles cardboard packed with sawdust, accept as customary fare the advertised "seven sweets and seven sours" that are more myth than reality on the Amish table, and go home again knowing little more about the Amish than they did before.

Tourists who do their homework find that "Pennsylvania Dutch" and "Amish" (pronounced AH-mish, not AM-ish, or AY-mish) are not synonymous. Many of the early settlers of Pennsylvania came from Germany at the invitation of William Penn, and the dialect that is common to most is a German dialect—not Dutch at all, but *Deutsch,* meaning German. Many of those early settlers were farmers. Most were Protestant. The Amish represent one of the Anabaptist sects who came from Germany at about the same time. Although they are of similar racial stock, the Amish call all non-Amish—even those of the same German background—"English." There are similarities with these "English" in language, in vocation, and in cooking, yet culturally they are divergent, for the Amish are shaped by their religious beliefs and the traditions that grow out of those beliefs and their German-"English" neighbors are not. These "English" are the Pennsylvania Dutch who permit hex signs on their farms (the Amish do not) and whose ancestors decorated useful items such as furniture and dishes, as well as manuscripts and documents, called *fracturs,* with colorful peasant-style designs. Products of Amish craftsmen are competent but plain.

Samuel Beiler is a fictitious but typical character, like all the characters in this book, though his last name—like the others used—is a real one, common to the area. He lives near Bird-in-Hand, six miles east of Lancaster. It is estimated that there are about sixty thousand Amish in the United States, about eighty percent of them concentrated in Pennsylvania, Ohio, and Indiana, with a few scattered settlements in other mostly midwestern states. The Lancaster County settlement is the second largest, and it is the oldest, since the first members of the sect arrived in the fertile limestone valleys of southeastern Pennsylvania early in the eighteenth century and transformed it into the "Garden Spot of Pennsylvania" and one of the most productive farming areas of the country.

Roughly a thousand Amish families live in Leacock Township in the eastern part of Lancaster County, and a large number of them are named Beiler. There are only about a dozen family names among the Lancaster Amish, and three-quarters of the people have one of seven family names, in addition to Beiler, in various spellings. The small number of family names is evidence that the Amish are *endogamous,* always choosing their mates from within the sect. An Amish person who marries outside the sect, or even into a more liberal branch of the sect, is placed under the *Meidung* and shunned for life. Because the horse and buggy is their sole method of private transportation (although they may use buses and hire taxis), the mobility of Amish young people is limited, and so is their choice of mates. The result is a high degree of intermarriage—not between first cousins, which is forbidden, but among families with a common, if distant, ancestor.

Since most Amish first names are drawn from the Bible, there is a great similarity among first as well as last names. Most women—88.3 percent—have one of twenty popular names; most men, about eighty percent, also have one of twenty names. To avoid confusion the Amish have an elaborate system of nicknaming, based on anything that helps to distinguish one Samuel Beiler from half a dozen others: middle initial—Sam Z; mother's name—Becky Sam; geographical origin—Leola Sam; or some personal quirk—Gravy Sam.

The Amish are, generally, friendly and hospitable people. Their attitudes toward outsiders vary with the individual and the circumstances. Tape recorders and cameras are not welcome, but a visitor sincerely interested in the Amish people who does not act like an interrogator can learn something about their way of life.

But not much. Amish society is complex and multi-level. The Amish live very much the way they did two hundred years ago. But it is not a changeless life, although change comes very slowly. The outsider sees horses and buggies riding dangerously on the highway and teams of horses slowly working the fields, but is puzzled by the news that some young men hide cars in the village while some bearded fathers appear behind the wheel. The visitor sees odd, old-fashioned clothes and mustacheless beards, but doesn't notice the presence or absence of buttons, the varying lengths of hair, the varying widths of hat brim, and other subtle distinctions among Amish groups. The outsider goes to see a "real Amish schoolhouse," operated strictly for the tourist, but may not notice the inconspicuous building on a back road where eight grades of children are taught by an Amish teacher. Perhaps aware that there was for years an "Amish school problem" when Amish parents were jailed for refusing to send their children to public school, the visitor is unsure of how the controversy was resolved, if indeed it was.

What a visitor can learn in talking with the Amish is that they are people living in the twentieth century: they have not escaped. They are concerned with the problems that worry anyone else: earning a living, preserving their personal freedom, raising and educating their children. They are also committed to preserve their eighteenth-century rural European traditions and to adapt them as functional instruments of survival in the twentieth century.

Sarah Beiler watches a car drive up the long lane from the public road and park at the end of the front walk. Three years ago Samuel nailed a hand-lettered sign, "Quilts for sale," on the post by the mailbox at the end of the lane. Tourists venturing from the overpowering commercialism of Route 30 toward the quieter, more rural Route 340 often see the sign and stop to examine the quilts Sarah's mother has for sale and, she knows well enough, to examine the home of a "real Amish family."

The living room is full of quilts made by Annie Beiler and her sisters, and lately some of their other relatives. The tourists come from the big cities, from New York and Philadelphia and Baltimore and Pittsburgh and even farther away to see how the Amish live. And they like to take home souvenirs. Annie learned that many of the "English" women like bright-colored patchwork quilts, and she began making them to sell. Sarah's father does not like the idea; it brings too many "English" to the house, and it seems that Annie is spending too much time at it and is perhaps not staying as close to the traditional woman's role as she should. But they need the money, and so far no one in the church has complained.

Sarah likes to see the tourists in their big cars and their bright clothes and jewelry, but she does not like to talk to them. They ask her too many questions, and sometimes they try to take her picture. Once she had to rescue her little sister Katie from them; the husband was trying to

Even a very young boy can handle a team of horses. MICHAEL RAMSEY

photograph his wife with the child, a miniature of her mother and older sisters, and Katie began to howl. They offered to pay Sarah if she would hold the tiny girl, but Sarah grabbed her and ran for the house. She could hear the camera clicking as she ran.

In the summer there are a lot of tourists. Most of them are nice, and they admire the quilts and often buy them. At the end of summer Annie moves aside the quilts that are left over and sets up the frame to make more quilts for the next season, working every evening until it is time to go to bed. Annie has taught Hannah, the oldest daughter, how to make the tiny running stitches, and Hannah has taught Sarah. They work until Sarah's eyes swim and her head aches. Her mother thinks it might be time for her to get glasses. All winter long they stitch and stitch, when the other work of stripping the tobacco and taking care of the animals is finished. When the tourists begin coming up the lane again in the summer, there will be plenty for them to choose from. Sometimes they quilt the tops that other women have pieced. Annie's sisters make some, and Annie is always looking for women who want her to sell their quilts for them.

The house in which the Beiler family lives is typically Amish: spacious and uncluttered, with a large kitchen and removable partitions in the walls that separate the rooms. About once a year, when it is their turn, the church district to which Annie and Jacob belong holds the Sunday preaching service in their house. The partitions are folded back, furniture moved aside, Annie's quilts packed away, and the district's benches are brought in and set up in rows. For that one Sunday morning the entire district fills the big house, singing hymns, praying, listening to the preaching, and staying on for a hearty lunch.

Annie Beiler is forty-five years old, but her age is difficult to guess. She is plump. Her brown hair, partially hidden by a white organdy cap, shows no sign of gray. There is no makeup on her smooth skin; she wears rimless glasses; her dress comes well below her knees. She could be thirty or fifty or anywhere in between.

While Sarah puts the water glasses on the table, her mother ushers the customer into the living room where bright-patterned quilts hang on clotheslines stretched across the room. Pillows and folded quilts and small handmade items are stacked on tables and in boxes. Annie enjoys these visitors, and she likes to answer their questions about how the quilts were made and who made them. The customer feels the prices are high; because the quilts were made by the Amish, whom she assumes, incorrectly, to be naive about the economics of the world, she expects them to be cheap. There are others who sell at lower prices, Annie tells her dubious customer, but they are not of this quality. Annie shows how the backing is made, pointing out the fineness of the stitches. The customer leaves at last, to think about it, promising to come back the next day before she returns home to New York. She wants her husband to see the quilts and to help her decide.

While the customer pondered, Annie's husband, Jacob Beiler, has come in from the fields. Jacob is two years older than his wife. His age, too, is hard to determine. His arms and hands are work-hardened; his face tanned and furrowed, while his beard and his hair, combed straight back from his forehead, are grizzled.

Hannah, the oldest daughter, returns from work soon after the customer leaves. She works at a greenhouse a few miles from her parents' farm. Her employer, who is not Amish, picks her up in the morning, along with a few other Amish employees, and drives her home in the late afternoon. Although they may not own or drive cars, there are no restrictions against riding with a non-Amish person.

Samuel thinks his sisters are lucky. Hannah, who is twenty, will probably be marrying soon. And until she does, she works away from home, not right under their father's nose. His brother John, the eldest of the children, married last winter. Although Hannah never speaks of it —no one ever talks about "dates" or "boyfriends"—Sam knows that Reuben Stoltzfus has been bringing her home from the Sunday evening singings. And he calls on her late Saturday night, as is the custom, after the rest of the family has gone to bed and the couple is completely alone. Frequently Sam sees Reuben leaving as he gets home, sometimes from a girl's house, more often from riding around in Ben's beautiful blue car. Reuben and Sam pretend not to notice each other.

And Sarah, at fifteen, is much different than Samuel was at that age. Girls do not seem to have the same feelings that boys do, Sam is quite sure, wanting cars and other worldly things. They seem more contented to stay

at home. Samuel was relieved when school was over for
him at the end of eighth grade, but Sarah enjoyed school
and showed a considerable flair for her studies. Sarah
cried when it ended and she knew there was no possibility
of continuing. Amish schools go only as far as the eighth
grade, and Amish children are not sent to public school.
The school all the Beiler children had attended is taught
by a young Amish woman who has not gone beyond the
eighth grade herself. But she is good with the children,
and she is quite capable of rehearsing her pupils in reading, writing, and arithmetic. The *real* education for their
lives, Sarah's parents believe, takes place at home, on the
farm. And that's where Sarah is needed. In a year or so,
when Amos and Elam are older and able to help more
and Katie is not underfoot so much, she can go out and
get a job like Hannah's.

But in the meantime, there is much to do at home.
With the rest of the family, Sarah works in the tobacco
fields, helping to plant the seedlings in the spring, to hoe
the acres of tobacco plants in the summer, to cut the
tobacco in the late summer and early fall, to strip the dry
leaves from the stalks in the winter. Sarah also has to help
her brother with the barn chores and her mother with the
family garden and the cooking. Sarah likes to bake.
Annie says Sarah's *schnitz* pies—made with dried apple
slices—will help her to get a good husband someday.

Sometimes Sarah likes to think ahead to the days when
she will have a young man coming to see her, like Hannah's Reuben. So far there is nobody special. Samuel takes
her to the Sunday night singings, and there is always

someone to bring her home; Samuel sees to that, so that he can be off with his friends. All the boys take their sisters, but it isn't their business to take their sisters home again. Sarah worries about Sam. He seems so wild. She knows that he wants a car and that he sneaks into movies when he gets a chance. He says that after he is baptized, he will settle down. But she knows that her father is talking to him about being baptized soon, and Samuel keeps avoiding it. Sarah is afraid that he may not be baptized, or that even when he is he might not give up his wild ways. If that happened, he would surely be shunned, and then he would be lost to them forever.

Sarah is fond of her brothers and her older sister, but her favorite in the family is four-year-old Katie. Sarah made her a doll of corn husks, and she takes her for rides in the boys' wagon. She spends even more time with her since their mother has been busy with the quilts. Sarah looks forward to the day when her new sister-in-law, John's wife Leah, will have her baby. It will not be long. Sarah really loves babies.

When the Beiler family sits down to the supper table, there are eight. Until last winter there were nine, but John, the eldest, married in the winter and is share-farming near New Holland. Samuel misses him most, even though they see him every other weekend. Amos is eight and Elam is twelve, and although they are both in school most of the day, for nine months a year, they have their chores to do before they leave and when they get home. Elam is very good with the animals. Amos has the chore of helping his mother in the kitchen, a job that he does not like at all. He would prefer to be out in the fields with his father and brother.

Jacob takes his place at the head of the table with Amos and Elam and Samuel on his right, and Annie on his left with Katie between them, and then Sarah and Hannah. The platters and bowls of food are set at the head of the table, in front of Jacob. After they have bowed their heads for silent prayer, Jacob helps himself and passes the serving dishes to his sons. They fill their plates with beef boiled with noodles and potatoes, pickled red beets and hard-boiled eggs, cole slaw, bread with cottage cheese and apple butter, and a rhubarb pie to finish the meal. Annie helps Katie with her food, and Hannah gets up to refill the dishes from the pots on the stove.

There is little conversation during the meal. When they are finished eating, there is another silent prayer, and the family disperses. The women clean up the kitchen, washing the dishes and putting away the left-over food in the kerosene-operated refrigerator. A one-cylinder engine in the cellar chugs noisily, powering the water pump.

After the kitchen chores are done and Katie has been put to bed, the rest of the family begins weeding the garden. They work until darkness sends them inside. The family goes to bed early, because the day begins at five o'clock.

While he works his way between rows of tomato plants, Samuel's mind returns again to his dilemma. He likes the

Acres of tobacco plants must be hoed by hand. CAROLYN MEYER

work of farming even though it is hard. He is glad that he is strong, and he likes to show what a good job he can do. Along with the responsibilities of growing up have come the privileges: At sixteen, when he reached the age of *Rum schpringe*—"running around"—Sam was given his own horse and his own open buggy which the "English" call a "bachelor buggy."

But he wishes he could get along better with his father. Jacob is a stern man, much stricter about everything than Sam's jovial mother. At first Sam could hardly wait to be doing the field work, carrying his own weight, side by side with his father. Now they are side by side, all right, but they rarely speak. Unless, it seems, Jacob is bawling Samuel out for something. Sam wonders what his father was like as a young man. Surely he was restless then, too. Sam has heard it said that the wilder the boys are when they're young, the stricter and more traditional they become when they're older. His father must have been a terror! When Jacob does speak, it is often on the subject of baptism. After he is baptized, Sam's life will change completely. Baptism carries with it the full responsibility of membership in the church, and then he will really have to settle down. Sam has seen it happen to his brother John: first baptism, then marriage, and now a baby on the way. There can be no turning back from any of that. If he can delay the baptism for a while longer, he will still have a little freedom, and maybe he can figure out a way to get himself a car.

From early childhood Samuel has been raised to be a farmer. Nearly all Amish men are farmers, except for those few who have related occupations—carpenters or millers. Some day he will have his own farm, and he'll live on it and work it and squeeze a living from it by constant effort, the way his father does. For Samuel, the options are closed, although he is not ignorant of them. He has sneaked off to see a few movies, and he sometimes manages to arrive at certain non-Amish neighbors' homes in the evening when the television is likely to be turned on. All of this is strictly forbidden. The church fathers can do nothing to punish him until he is baptized, but they can try hard to influence him by putting pressure on his father. And he knows what that can mean: his father does not yet believe his seventeen-year-old son is too old for a "smacking" with a buggy whip. And so Samuel is careful, very careful. And he thinks, sometimes, about leaving for good.

But Samuel Beiler is Amish. At seventeen, he is an experienced farmer. In a few years he will, like most of his friends—even most of the wild ones—have a quiet Amish wife, a farm of his own, and several little "woodchoppers" and "dishwashers" to lend a hand in accomplishing the enormous amount of work there is to be done without benefit of the usual laborsaving gadgets. Samuel's life is planned for him; it is settled and secure, and when it comes right down to it, he probably will not trade it for anything "the world" has to offer.

And yet, he would give a lot—maybe not everything, but certainly a lot—to own a car.

SYMBOLS

Separation From
an Evil World

KATIE BEILER, dressed like a miniature of her mother, perches between her parents on the front seat of the family buggy. Amos and Elam ride in the back of the buggy, watching where they have been instead of where they're going. They, too, are dressed in their best clothes, similar to their father's, for the Sunday preaching at Abram Riehl's farm.

Like the habits worn by a religious order, the quaint, picturesque clothes Katie and her family wear and the clothing of all Amish people symbolize their nonconformity—their separation from "the world." Subtle differences tell the Amish a great deal about each other; each detail is dictated by the *Ordnung* of the church district.

24

Katie's dress is royal blue; her mother's is rich brown. Katie likes bright colors, but pinks, reds, and yellows are forbidden and so are patterned fabrics. Her sister Sarah sewed the plain dress for her, the same one-piece style worn by all Amish women regardless of age: long straight sleeves, full skirt hemmed halfway between knees and ankles, high collarless neck, top fastened shut in front with straight pins or hooks and eyes. Buttons are forbidden; so are safety pins. Over their shoulders the women wear the *Holsz duuch,* a triangular shawl pinned in front and back to the waistband of an apron, which is also pinned. (Apron strings tied in a bow would be considered frivolous and are, therefore, also forbidden.) In the back of the dress at the waistline of the women and older girls there is a small tab called a *Lepli.* Neither Annie nor her daughters can explain its significance; it has simply always been there.

Katie, and her sisters who are riding with Samuel in his open buggy, all wear white aprons and white shawls for the Sunday preaching. Annie and the other married women wear aprons and shawls in colors that match their dresses. They wear black stockings, rolled below the knee, and black low-heeled oxfords. Katie is not happy about the shoes. In warm weather at home, the whole family goes barefoot.

Almost since the time she was born, Katie has worn the devotional cap, a white organdy head covering. Hannah and Sarah, like the other unmarried girls over the age of twelve, change to a black cap for the Sunday preaching. After they are married, they will wear the white cap

all the time. The head coverings look virtually identical
to the outsider, but like the caps worn by nurses, there are
variations that convey information: the width of the
front part, the length of the ties, the style of the seams,
and the presence of laboriously ironed pleats signify where
the woman lives and how conservative or liberal her
church district is.

Under the neat cap, Katie's hair is parted in the middle
and plaited over her ears, and the tiny braids are fastened
in the back. (Amish women never cut or curl their hair
or let it hang loose. When Katie is grown she will pin her
hair in a plain knot at the back of her neck.) Over the
cap, Katie wears a small version of her mother's black
bonnet that some writers describe as a "candle-snuffer"
with its deep scoop brim.

The way Jacob Beiler dresses is just as carefully prescribed by the *Ordnung*. For Sunday preaching, he wears
a *Mutze,* a long black frock coat with split tails and hook-
and-eye closings. It has neither collar nor lapels. Under it
is a vest, also fastened with hooks and eyes. Some people
believe buttons are forbidden because the Amish are
pacifists and feel that buttons are of military origin. Another explanation is that buttons are banned because they
are decorative. Whatever the basis, the rule seems to the
outsider to be remarkably inconsistent, for while buttons
are strictly forbidden on some clothes, they are acceptable
on others.

Jacob's broadfall, or "barn-door," trousers have no fly;
a wide front flap buttons along the sides as sailors' bell-
bottom trousers once did. No creases and no belt; home-

made suspenders hold up Jacob's pants. There are buttons on his shirt, the number specifically stipulated by the *Ordnung.* Colored shirts are permitted, but stripes and prints are not. Neckties are forbidden.

When Jacob is not dressed for the preaching, he replaces his *Mutze* with a *Wamus,* a black sack coat simply cut with either high round neck or V-neck and neither lapels nor outside pockets. Sometimes the *Wamus* has hooks and eyes, but more liberal church districts allow buttons. Buttoned sweaters are sometimes permitted. There are also buttons on the long greatcoats donned by some of the older men in cold weather, when most of the younger ones simply add more layers of clothing.

In winter Jacob and the other men and boys wear broad-brimmed black felt hats; in summer they switch to straw. The hat is a kind of status symbol among the Amish. Elam and Amos have been wearing hats with brims a bit wider than three inches since they were even younger than Katie. Their oldest brother, John, wears a hat with a crease around the top of the crown, the sign— together with his sprouting beard—of a newly married man. Their grandfather's hat is higher in the crown than Jacob's, and his brim is four inches wide. The bishop who will preach at the Sunday service is easily recognized—by Amish people—by his high, rounded crown and the broadest brim in the district.

The width of an Amish hat brim not only signifies his status in the district but also his degree of orthodoxy. The broader the brim, the more conservative the wearer, and the less amenable he is to change. Young rebels like Samuel's cousin Ben sometimes trim their hat brims to just a little less than the prescribed width. Too much trimming can precipitate a visit to the boy's parents by church officials; he will not be baptized unless his hat brim conforms to the *Ordnung* of the district.

Jacob Beiler's long beard is as much a mark of his Amishness as his broad-brimmed hat. He shaves only his upper lip, since mustaches are against the rules. Jacob and all his sons cut their hair straight around, well below the ears. Amos and Elam have theirs parted in the middle with bangs across the forehead. Samuel, encouraged by his cousin Ben's example but not brave enough to trim his hat brim, demonstrated his independence and rebelliousness by chopping his thick brown hair right up to the earlobe. His father was furious but there was little he could do except wait for it to grow in again.

When the Amish first began to arrive in the American colonies early in the eighteenth century, they wore what others of their social and economic class were wearing: knee breaches for the men, wide-brimmed flat-crowned hats for the women, the costume of rural folk left "plain," without any decoration. It was not until about a hundred years ago that the current clothing styles were adopted, and, among the Old Order Amish, they have changed very little since.

Annie and the girls make most of the clothes for the family. They sew all of their own dresses and shawls and aprons and bonnets. They also sew the pants and straight-cut jackets for Amos and Elam and the work clothes for the men. When Samuel turned sixteen, the family visited

A gray-bearded farmer sports his summer straw hat. GERALD DODDS

a department store in New Holland, a village northeast
of Bird-in-Hand. Annie bought plain solid-colored fabric
for dresses for the girls and shirts for the boys, as well as
the bright-patterned fabric she uses for the quilts. Jacob
ordered a new *Mutze,* shaking his head over the price,
which was higher than for "worldly" suits because setting
in the hooks and eyes is a much more difficult tailoring
job than sewing buttons and making buttonholes. "Plain"
doesn't necessarily mean inexpensive.

As is customary for a boy who has reached the age for
"running around," or dating, they had Samuel fitted for
his first store-bought suit. Samuel was pleased, but he
wished his parents would leave him alone in the store for
a few minutes so he could browse through the racks of
"worldly" clothes. He knew that some of his friends had
hidden caches of forbidden clothes—as well as cars—and
bragged about managing a complete change of identity,
whenever they wanted. Samuel in his broad-brimmed hat
dreams of someday outfitting himself in clothes likes theirs
and being mistaken for an *Englischer.*

The buggy in which Jacob Beiler is driving his family
to the preaching is quite new. Black with a gray top and
iron tires on the big wooden wheels, as prescribed by the
Ordnung, it looks exactly like the old one that he had had
since he was first married. Despite the battery-powered
side lamps, reflectors, and bright orange triangles added
as required by Pennsylvania state law, Jacob's old carriage had not been noticed by the driver of an automobile
one rainy night until it was too late to swerve or stop, and

the carriage was demolished. Fortunately, Jacob emerged shaken but unscathed. Often Amish buggies, dark, slow-moving, and nearly invisible on the road at night, are involved in fatal accidents.

Within a few days after the accident, Jacob placed his order for a new buggy with the Amish carriage maker. When Jacob bought his first buggy, carriage-making was a non-Amish occupation, but increased demand created by the growing Amish population and the toll of wrecked carriages, together with the need for approved work in addition to farming, has brought some Amish into the trade. Even so, the waiting list for handmade buggies is long. For nearly a year the family had to make do with the market wagon and Samuel's one-seated open "bachelor buggy."

During those months of waiting, Jacob stopped by often to check on the progress of his and other buggies and, in spite of himself, to admire the array of power tools, allowed for use in his business by the carriage maker's more liberal church district. The big wheels were precisely set, toed in slightly with the tops a bit farther apart than the bottoms, and a gear assembly at the pivot of the front axle to add stability to the vehicle with a high center of gravity. The brakes are simple: an iron block, operated by hand, presses hard against the rear iron buggy tire. This kind of brake is prescribed by the *Ordnung;* different kinds of brakes are permitted in different groups, where the *Ordnung* also tells the buggy owner whether or not he may have a dashboard, a whipsocket, and other variations. In other parts of the country, he may be required to have a yellow top on his buggy, or a white top, or a black top, or no top at all. Jacob authorized one change in his new carriage: the old one had roll-up side curtains, but the new one has glass windows in front and sliding side doors with windows. The buggy, when it was finished, cost more than a thousand dollars. His driving horse had not been injured in the read-end collision, but if Jacob had had to replace him, it would have cost him at least five hundred dollars; a new harness would have added another one hundred and fifty dollars.

Driving briskly toward Abram Riehl's farm behind Chester's familiar chestnut rump, Jacob Beiler admires again the fine handling of his new carriage and marvels that anyone could think an automobile is better.

Above the clatter of shod hooves and the rumble of the wheels on the blacktop road, Katie jabbers to her mother, who answers briefly, in deference to the silent Jacob. The language they speak is Pennsylvania Dutch, a German dialect related to and derived from the dialects spoken in the southwestern section of Germany from which the Amish forefathers came. It is primarily a spoken language, and spelling varies considerably, according to the writer. Some scholars prefer to call the dialect "Pennsylvania German."

No matter what name the scholars bestow, Pennsylvania Dutch is the language Katie and her family and all Amish speak among themselves. Although a large number of people of German descent in Pennsylvania speak the dialect, only among the Amish is Pennsylvania Dutch the "mother tongue." It is another mark of Amish refusal to conform to the ways of the world.

Katie does not yet know any English, but in a few years, when she starts to school, she will learn to speak as well as to read and write in the language of "the world." The Amish want their children to have fluency in English, because they depend for their survival on good business relationships with English-speaking people—whether it's selling quilts or tobacco, buying clothes or fertilizer.

Sometimes when the Amish converse in English, they fall back on German word order or Pennsylvania Dutch idioms translated literally into English. The results are the quaint expressions that delight and amuse tourists and inspire the makers of "Amish" souvenirs to decorate switchplates with "Outen the light" or "Make the light out" and letter cocktail napkins and note paper with "typical" expressions like "Come here once," "Throw Papa down the stairs his hat," "The soup is wonderful hot," "The milk is all" (meaning all gone), and "It's making down hard" (raining). The borrowing works both ways; the English of non-Amish Pennsylvanians sometimes absorbs a few "Dutch" words; uncombed hair is "stroobly"; a badly-done job is "all booghered up"; a careless person is "schooslich."

At about the same time that Katie Beiler starts to learn English, she will also be taught High German, the language of religion. The family Bible is written in High German, and she must learn to read it. By the time she is baptized in her late teens, Katie will be able to understand most of the Sunday sermon and to join in the pray-

ers and hymns. Because the Amish pronounce and inflect
High German as though it were Pennsylvania Dutch, it
is usually called "Amish High German."

Katie will learn High German, her third language, in
school. Years ago when Amish children attended public
schools where German was not part of the curriculum,
parents had the responsibility of teaching their children
the religious language at home, reading with them from
the Bible on Sunday afternoons. Most Amish cannot converse in High German and have no reason to acquire such
fluency unless they are ordained church officials who must
preach sermons and pray. But understanding is of great
importance to everyone.

When they arrive at the Riehls' farm, Katie holds
tightly to her mother's hand and enters the farm house
for the long service that will require her to be both silent
and still for several hours. The language is incomprehen-
sible to her, but she is becoming aware that being there
and listening to that singsong speech is somehow at the
very heart of her family's life.

The preaching service over and their stomachs comfort-
ably full of Elizabeth Riehl's half-moon pies, Amos and
Elam Beiler have concluded that the best thing about
Sunday is the food. The worst thing is that Sunday is the
day before Monday, and that means school.

Amos, a third grader, says he really doesn't mind going
to school, but Elam does not share his brother's feelings.
Elam, who is in sixth grade, can hardly wait for school to

The extra-broad hat brim and the kerchief signify a conservative church district in Mifflin County, Pennsylvania. GERALD DODDS

be over. He would much rather be outside, working in the fields or doing almost anything than be shut up in the schoolhouse. He would gladly trade places with his older brothers and sisters, who don't have to be bothered about school any more. Sarah, who has just finished her schooling, says that school is very good and they should make the most of it. But, Elam claims, that is because Sarah is a girl. Katie, too, chatters constantly about going to school, although she has two more years to wait. Katie will not be sent to kindergarten, because the Amish believe that children should be at home with their parents until they are six.

Amish children go to school through eighth grade, or until they reach their fourteenth birthdays. The scholars, as school-age children are called, on the Beiler farm wake up with the rest of the family about five o'clock each morning and jump into their clothes in their unheated bedroom. Amos, who is eight, must see that the chickens and rabbits are clean and have enough feed and water. Elam, twelve years old, has cows to milk. After the chores are done, the family sits down to eat the hearty breakfast Annie has cooked: fried cornmeal mush, eggs, bread and butter with Hannah's strawberry jam, and pie left over from the night before. There is not much conversation, but Jacob tells Samuel about the work that must be done that day.

Amos and Elam help their mother clear away the breakfast dishes before they leave for school. They have a long walk—almost two miles. Whenever possible, schools are built to serve children within a two-mile radius, so that no one has to walk more than two miles.

Jacob Beiler helped to build the schoolhouse. Some of the children in the area attend old one-room schoolhouses that were once owned by the public school district. When districts consolidated and new modern buildings were erected, the Amish bought the obsolete schools and re-modeled them—not modernizing them but instead ripping out all the electric wiring and sometimes even lowering the high ceilings to make the atmosphere cozier. There was no such old schoolhouse available near Jacob's farm. Instead, the Amish fathers in the neighborhood got together and built their own, a simple, solid-looking structure of cinderblock, with big windows to take advantage of the natural light.

Promptly at half-past eight, Rebecca King pulls the rope on the old-fashioned bell on the roof. Amos and Elam like to get there as early as they can, so there is a little time to play ball before the bell rings. After Becky rings the bell—the pupils call her by her first name, as they do all adults, regardless of age—the children line up and file through the big front doors into the cloakroom. They hang their hats and jackets on pegs, line up their lunch boxes, and go quickly and quietly to their desks.

Stepping into an Amish school in the 1970s is like entering a time machine and emerging sixty or more years ago. Old-fashioned desks bought second hand and carefully refinished are arranged in neat rows, facing the teacher's desk at the front of the room. Next to her is a

"recitation bench." There are thirty-one students in the
eight grades Becky teaches, and each class of three or four
or five pupils comes forward by turns to sit on the bench
and recite its lessons.

The day begins with the roll call. Attendance is high in
the Amish school. If someone is absent, Becky and the
pupils are concerned, because the absence must mean illness. When the children attended public schools, a few
families sometimes insisted on keeping their children at
home when they needed them to help with the necessary
work. But now the Amish simply close down the schools for
a few days during the peak periods, and close earlier in the
spring than the public schools. They compensate for the
missed time by taking only a very short Christmas recess
and none of the usual national holidays. Either everyone
stays home to work, or everyone is in school to learn except in the case of illness.

After the roll call, Becky reads to the pupils from the
German Bible, and then all recite together the Lord's
Prayer in German. Amos and Elam and most of the others
had already learned the prayer before they started to
school, but some of the first graders still have difficulty.
Becky and the children speak English exclusively in the
classroom, except for the lessons in reading German scriptures and prayers.

Becky starts her students off with an arithmetic lesson.
Arithmetic is considered very important, because it is essential to the work of any farmer; he must know enough
of it to operate his farm efficiently, like any small busi-

ness. After the first graders have had ten minutes or so to review their lessons, the second graders take their places on the recitation bench. Amos goes forward with the other third graders to practice subtraction. Becky holds up flash cards with each problem. "Nine take away five?" The pupils answer together: "Four." There is no competition for one to come up with the answer more quickly than another. In a little while, Elam's sixth grade will work on long division, writing the figures on the slate blackboard behind Becky's desk. While each class is reciting, the others work on their arithmetic assignments at their desks. If there's time before recess, the whole school will recite the multiplication tables in chorus. The young ones absorb a little from the older ones, and even those who have presumably passed on to more demanding disciplines benefit from the review. Besides, all of them seem to enjoy the singsong of the chorus.

During the fifteen-minute morning recess, the boys immediately resume their baseball game, picking up where they left off the day before. Elam is the first baseman; all the prime positions are taken by the older boys, but Becky makes sure the smaller ones are included, too. That's one of the rules of the Amish schoolyard: children are never allowed to stand around by themselves; everyone must be included in the group. The older girls are playing blindman's bluff; the younger ones are racing around in a game of tag, and it is this game that Becky joins. During recess and lunchtime, the yard is filled with shouts and conversation in both English and Pennsylvania Dutch and some-

Shoes come off but prayer caps stay in place when girls play ball at recess. MICHAEL RAMSEY

times a mixture. There has been some disagreement among parents about which language should be used in the schoolyard. More pragmatic parents want their children to develop as much fluency as possible in English, but other, more tradition-minded parents contend that the use of English when it's not absolutely necessary helps to drive a wedge between the Amish child and the Amish community. Becky takes a middle course. She encourages the younger ones to speak English when they play, but the older ones who have demonstrated mastery of English may use Pennsylvania Dutch.

The fifteen minute recess period passes quickly. Elam has caught a fly ball for the final out for his team, and at lunchtime he will be at bat. He intends to slug the ball far out into a farmer's cornfield and enjoy the sight of his little brother and friends hunting for the ball.

Back in the schoolroom, the children settle down quickly to reading, a subject they all seem to enjoy. The task of selecting books for the pupils was not simple, for the parents want the subject matter to be about farm children, not about city life; they want the stories to teach a moral lesson; fairy tales, myths, and fantasies are taboo. Most modern readers are thought to be too worldly, showing families with elaborate wardrobes and too many material possessions. As a result, the books they use would be considered hopelessly outdated by teachers and pupils in most public schools who would probably be dismayed by most Amish educational materials and teaching methods. But it is important to remember that Amish values are quite different from the values of the rest of American society. The Amish want their children to learn to work together as a group, not to compete as individuals. Preserving tradition is a goal; learning to reason abstractly is not. This concept begins to take hold in early childhood; even little Katie has learned that asking "too many" questions is not acceptable. And so, rather than stimulating their pupils with as wide a variety of experiences as possible, the Amish offer a very limited range, and they expect the pupils to master that material unquestioningly. Memorization replaces reasoning in a culture dominated by oral tradition. Fast learning is not considered a virtue; thoroughness is more important. Parents and teachers are no more impressed with a child's intellectual gifts than they are with physical attributes. Elam has never been much of a student; he is, actually, a slow learner. But Amos is very bright, and if he were a non-Amish child in a non-Amish school, he would probably be placed in an advanced group and get an enriched curriculum or an accelerated program. Jacob and Annie do not believe that Amos's quickness will make him a more efficient farmer; his teacher believes that his talents are a gift from God, and she encourages him to use the gift by helping others in the school. And Jacob has said that Elam will probably remember his times-tables longer, because he has been so slow in mastering them.

Lunchtime never seems to come soon enough for Amos and Elam. Hannah packs their lunchboxes when she fixes her own to take with her to the greenhouse, and the boys always look forward to discovering what she has put in for them. Elam dotes on liverwurst sandwiches, especially when the bread is homemade and sliced thick. In winter there is always a container of soup, which the children heat on the woodstove in the middle of the room. There is a slice of pie—they are made quite firm, so they can be eaten out of hand—or a piece of cake or a few fresh cookies or sticky cinnamon buns. The long-awaited lunch is consumed in about ten minutes; Elam sees no point in wasting precious time in eating when he can be out playing baseball. The game takes up where it left off, but Amos declines to join. He and some of the younger boys have decided to let the bigger boys chase their own high flies; they would rather play dodge ball.

By the time Becky rings the afternoon bell, clouds have begun to pile up in the west. Most of the children notice and comment; like all farmers, they are closely attuned to changes in the weather. When afternoon recess comes, it is raining hard, and no one can go outside. Becky distributes the game boards. Elam challenges his friend Crist to checkers and Amos joins three girls for Parcheesi. And then it's back to work again.

Discipline in the Amish classroom is strict. Through the long busy day, the only voices are those of Becky King and the pupils who are reciting. Yet, despite the apparent rigidity, the quiet, and the orderly rows of desks, the Amish schoolroom is an example of an effective "open classroom." There are all ages, all levels of intelligence and achievements, and the children take responsibility for each other, older children helping younger ones, faster learners coaching the slower ones.

Before the day ends, there is time for singing. Most

Amish children like to sing and singing is a vital part of the Amish tradition. It is important in their religious life, and in their social life as well. There are no harmonized part-songs for the Amish of any age; unaccompanied unison singing is universally prescribed by the *Ordnung*. The Amish have their own style of singing, in which the leader sings the first word and is joined for the rest of the line by the group. Elam seems to have a good natural ear and has shown a special talent for leading. Amos is pleased when his brother Elam leads the singing, and he looks forward to the day when Elam might take the role of *Vorsänger* at the Sunday preaching.

At half-past three the children are dismissed. The rain has stopped, but before they can leave, the children sweep out the room, make sure desks are neatly in line, books put away, all papers, having been used as much as possible, thrown in the wastebasket, blackboards—old-fashioned slate, not the green chalkboards of the newer schools —washed and the erasers clapped together until they are clean. The children take care of all the janitorial work. When cold weather comes, they will help to carry in the wood for the stove, and they will take turns cleaning out the ashes and banking the fire for the next day.

The school chores finished, Amos and Elam put on their hats, pick up their lunchboxes, and start home, where more chores must be done before their mother calls them for supper.

The Amish accept the idea of sending their children to school for eight years in order to learn what they need to know to survive in the twentieth-century rural economy. But the really important things an Amish child needs to know to survive in the Amish culture he learns from his parents and from other adults in the community. Katie, at the age of four, is learning what it is to be an Amish woman by observing her mother and her sisters. The boys are learning what it is to be Amish men by watching and imitating their father. School gives them a few of the necessary skills, but most of the practical knowledge of being farmers and housewives is acquired not in books but in a kind of family apprenticeship: the boys are trained to repair machinery, take care of animals, help with carpentry projects, and work in the fields; the girls learn about cooking, sewing, washing and ironing, growing vegetables, and budgeting. All experience the cycle of the farmer's year and learn to dovetail special projects with daily chores and seasonal demands.

For years public school authorities were in conflict with the Amish. There were many unpleasant incidents when truancy laws were enforced by school districts unwilling to lose state subsidies based on attendance; Amish fathers were often arrested and jailed for refusing to send their older children to school. Various solutions to the "school question" were attempted: in 1955 Pennsylvania officials worked out a compromise, a way of keeping Amish children within the boundaries of compulsory attendance laws without violating Amish religious beliefs.

Until Samuel observed his fifteenth birthday, he was enrolled in an Amish vocational school for three hours each Saturday. Sam and about two dozen other students who had finished eighth grade when Amish belief requires them to end their schooling, but who had not reached their fifteenth birthday, when the state would issue them a farm permit and allow them to leave school, met to sing a few songs, recite the Lord's Prayer in German, study hygiene, social studies, more advanced English and arithmetic than they learned in regular school, and—most important—to work on their journals, the record each student kept of the work done on the farm each day of the week.

But not every state was so sympathetic or so innovative. Unresolved problems in Wisconsin were brought before the United States Supreme Court, which ruled in 1972 that the Amish sect is exempt from state compulsory education laws requiring a child to attend beyond the eighth grade, claiming that such laws violate the Constitutional right to the freedom of religion. Chief Justice Warren Burger, pointing out the centuries-old resistance of the Amish, stressed that the exemption cannot be granted to new sects or communes that decide to reject formal education. Justice William O. Douglas filed a partial dissent, expressing concern for the number of Amish youths who drift away from the faith (he puts the figure at one-third to one-half) and are not educationally equipped for "the world."

Although the Supreme Court ruling freed the Amish from the compulsory aspects of the weekly three-hour class and journal-keeping, the Amish have found it worth continuing. It was with a sigh of relief that Samuel completed his journal on his fifteenth birthday, but Sarah was as proud of her daily record of accomplishment as she is of the rows of canned wax beans and sour cherries on the shelf, and the stacks of patchwork pillows she has made for her mother to sell to the tourists. Both she and Samuel are well-educated for Amish life.

HISTORY

Sixteenth-Century Europe to Twentieth-Century America

S AMUEL BEILER smiles to himself. Someone has been taking his picture. Samuel has been harrowing the fields since early morning. Late in the afternoon, while the sun is still high, he watches the small white car moving slowly along the road at the edge of the field. The car stops, and out of the corner of his eye Samuel catches a glimpse of sunlight reflected on a camera lens.

The *Ordnung* does not allow photographs. Some say it it forbidden because it shows pride in one's appearance; others claim it has to do with making "graven images." But the picturesque Amish are nearly irresistible subjects for the non-Amish person with a camera and there are, in fact, several handsome collections of photographs of

49

Amish life captured by persistent photographers. In many pictures the subject is turned away from the camera, but many have obviously co-operated—if not exactly posed—for the picturetaking.

There is not much Samuel can do about the person in the car. Hannah would tell him to hold his hat over his face. But he keeps on moving slowly over the newly turned earth and lets the shutter click. Samuel, the unbaptized rebel, hopes the photographer has a telephoto lens to bring him into closer view. He wishes that someday he could see one of the pictures that are being taken of him.

Even with a series of fine pictures, the photographer carries away no more understanding of Amish beliefs and tradition than the casual tourist who eats shoofly pie or buys one of Annie's quilts. The roots that nourish Amish beliefs and bring vitality to Amish tradition extend back hundreds of years, a complex story of persecution from without and division within. Remembrance of the past is a part of the daily present for every Amish person and is not relegated to Sunday worship and occasional ceremonial observances.

It seemed to many people in Europe in the sixteenth century—just as it does to many people today—that the world was in a terrible state. And so it was: the poor, who were in the majority by far, were exploited and made miserable by the rich and powerful few. The Roman Catholic Church wielded tremendous influence at the time, and many people blamed the Church for the ills of society. The time was ripe for rebirth and reform.

History books traditionally focus on Martin Luther and the Protestant Reformation, which was launched when in 1517 Luther, a Catholic priest, posted his historic ninety-five theses on the door of the castle church in Wittenburg, Germany. Luther was protesting the sale of indulgences, by which the believer received relief from punishment for his sins. He argued that salvation should come from the faith of the believer. Luther had a wide following, but he lost much of it during the Peasants' War, when in 1524 the exploited peasants of southern Germany, near the Swiss border, rose up in revolt. Luther's harsh stand against them helped to crush the rebellion within two years.

Luther had many opponents besides the Roman Catholic Church. It was a time of ferment with various factions arising in reaction to each other. In another parallel to our present age, it was also a time of cults, including devil-worshippers, charismatic Christians, and communes where wives were shared as well as goods.

The first major figure to break with Luther was Ulrich Zwingli, a radical Swiss Protestant, who differed with Luther over interpretation of the Lord's Supper, as the Reformers called the Eucharist or Holy Communion. But Zwingli was, in turn, opposed by Conrad Grebel, who felt that Zwingli was straying too far from the Bible as the sole basis of authority. Zwingli favored infant baptism and a state church. Grebel and his followers wanted to establish free congregations of believers who were baptized as adults and who made a confession of faith and committed themselves freely to a Christian life. Zwingli had the support of the Great Council of Zurich, which announced that babies must be baptized within eight days after their birth, or the parents would be exiled.

The year was 1525 and marked the beginning of the Anabaptist movement, a term meaning "rebaptized" and applied derogatorily at the time. Anabaptism was regarded as radically left wing, a threat to both Roman Catholic and Protestant establishments. In the years that followed, Anabaptist leaders were beaten, tortured, drowned, burned at the stake, and killed by the sword, until by the end of the sixteenth century nearly all of the original Anabaptists of Switzerland and Germany had been put to death.

In spite of the intense persecution—or perhaps because of it—the Anabaptist movement spread through central and western Europe. In Holland, a former Roman Catholic priest named Menno Simons left the Church to become one of those hunted and persecuted for their Anabaptist preaching. His followers became known first as Mennists, then as Mennonites, and the disliked nickname "Anabaptist" fell into disuse among the believers. The Mennonites of Switzerland also called themselves the Swiss Brethren.

As though it were not enough that they were hounded by Catholics, Lutherans, and Reformed groups, toward the end of the sixteenth century, dissension began to grow among the Mennonites themselves, not on matters of belief but on matters of practice. One principal source of disagreement was interpretation of the *Meidung,* the practice of shunning or avoiding a member of the church who had broken a rule. The basis for the *Meidung* is the Apostle Paul's advice to the Corinthians: "But now I have written unto you not to keep company, if any man that is called a brother be a fornicator, or covetous, or an idolater, or a railer, or a drunkard, or an extortioner; with such an one no not to eat." (1 Corinthians 5:11)

The Mennonites interpreted this to mean excommunication of the member who was to be subjected to *Meidung* only at communion. But Jakob Ammann, a young bishop of the Swiss Brethren in Bern, insisted that the *Meidung* had more far-reaching implications. Not only must the person under the ban be excluded from the communion table, but he should also be shunned at every other occasion; even his own family should refuse to speak to him or eat with him or have anything whatever to do with him until he repented and had been forgiven.

More liberal Mennonites pointed out that Christ, Himself, had eaten with publicans and sinners, and that shunning was to be spiritual, rather than actual. The controversy over *Meidung* grew, fueled by other questions of practice, and in 1697 the stubborn and fiery Jakob Ammann broke away from the Swiss Brethren Mennonites. His followers, known as the Amish, were as stubborn and inflexible as Ammann himself, and they became characterized by their unwillingness to change. Although differences in details of clothing were not a primary issue, they did become symbolic of the split. The Amish became known as the *Häftlers* (Hook-and-eyers), while the more worldly Mennonites were called the *Knöpflers* (Buttoners).

Meanwhile, life did not improve for the European peasants, especially those in the Rhenish Palatinate of southwest Germany. The Thirty Years' War in the first half of the seventeenth century made conditions worse, and even after the war ended, the burning and plundering went on. The farmer spent his life completely under the domination of the landlord, on the lowest rung of the social and economic ladder, scorned but essential to the power and prosperity of the wealthy nobility who exploited him. It would seem that the life of toil, the fruits of which were always claimed by the landowner, was hardly worth living.

And then came a chance to escape.

In 1681, King Charles II of England ridded himself of a debt to Sir William Penn by granting to Penn's son, also named William, a large province in the American colonies. A devout Quaker, the younger Penn had already suffered in England for his liberal avant-garde beliefs—being first expelled from Oxford and then banished to the Continent by his father in the classic cure for wrongheadedness. But as proprietor of the hilly, wooded lands in America, William Penn believed that he could offer refuge, freedom, and equality to the persecuted. He saw it as a "holy experiment."

The original settlers of the area—about two or three thousand of them—had been English, Dutch, and Swedish. When Penn arrived in 1682, he had the city of Philadelphia laid out as the capital and changed the name of the area from Penn's Woods to Pennsylvania. The following year Francis Daniel Pastorius arrived from Germany, representing the Frankfort Land Company, which had

*Carrying their shoes, a group of Amish pass the
dilapidated fence of an "English" farm.* MICHAEL RAMSEY

purchased land in Pennsylvania. Pastorius wrote glowing descriptions of the area to his friends at home, and soon the German immigration began, joining the influx of English Quakers. Various accounts show that the ocean voyages were difficult, with long months at sea, unpalatable food, and little water. Safely on American shores, the impoverished German immigrants were greeted by the people who paid for their crossings in return for years of servitude until the debt was discharged; only then could the immigrants begin the difficult task of clearing the land for their own use. "Redemptioners," as such immigrants were called, because their passage was a debt paid off or redeemed, were common in Colonial America. Shipowners, who knew the demand for cheap labor, profited greatly. Often the redemptioners were poorly treated and taken advantage of. To help them, an act was passed in 1700 providing each servant of four years or more with two suits of clothing—one new, one used—and an ax and two hoes to start his new, independent life.

Pastorius brought the first group of Mennonites to Pennsylvania and they established themselves in Germantown, northwest of Philadelphia, in 1683. Within six years of their arrival in America, these Mennonites had issued a protest against slavery—the first disapproval voiced in North America, predating Lincoln's Emancipation Proclamation by 174 years.

The first Amish immigrants left Switzerland and the Palatinate of Germany in 1727, joining the great migration of Germans to America. They settled originally near Hamburg, to the north of what is now the small city of

Reading, but Indian raids during the French and Indian War weakened that community. The Amish then moved toward the southwest. By the time of the Revolutionary War, about half of the 225,000 Pennsylvania colonists were German, most of them Lutheran or members of the Reformed churches. Only a small minority was Amish and Mennonite.

The large number of German settlers made the English-speaking colonists uneasy. Although the Germans, particularly the Amish, proved themselves to be excellent farmers, the English looked down upon them. Benjamin Franklin dismissed them as "stupid boors," and the English colonists established programs to attempt to Anglicize the children. The Germans, however, distrusted the motives of those who proposed to educate them. The plain sects, such as the Amish, were determined to hold on to their religion, which was a way of life that included their language, their plain ways of dressing, and their farming. And as early as the eighteenth century, they understood that "English" attempts to educate them were a threat to everything they considered sacred. It was a problem that was not satisfactorily resolved for nearly two centuries.

The Amish and the Mennonites have always been willing to migrate, moving in groups so that they can create cultural "islands" with a common language and philosophy. In 1767 the Amish settled in southwestern Pennsylvania; from there they spread to the midwestern states. The first Ohio settlement was established in 1807; Ohio now has eighty church districts and the largest Amish population in the United States. Indiana, with the third largest number of Amish, after Pennsylvania, was settled in 1842. (Eighty percent of all Amish church districts are located in these three states.) Settlements were being founded in Illinois, Iowa, Kansas, Oklahoma, and Wisconsin through the nineteenth and into the first decade of the twentieth century. Some Amish immigrants went directly from Germany to Ontario, Canada, in 1824.

As population pressure increases the demand for farm land, and as society's pressure increases the need for relative isolation, colonization has continued, but it has not always been successful. A group of families attempted to create a settlement in Mexico but failed; there were also groups of determined settlers in British Honduras and Paraguay in the 1960s who have managed to survive.

Before the middle of the nineteenth century, the Amish of Pennsylvania were all of one conservative mind. But beginning in 1850 and for the next three decades, there was a series of schisms. The first major division split the Amish into two main factions. The more progressive group accepted gradual change. Called Amish Mennonites, or "high Amish" because they were less "lowly," they built meeting houses which also earned them the name of "Church Amish," to distinguish them from the stricter "House Amish" who continued to worship in their homes. Since then there have been innumerable cleavages, all caused by different interpretations of the *Meidung,* as happened in the days of Jakob Ammann, or by different details of the *Ordnung*—by *Häftlers* who want to live like *Knöpflers* but still remain Amish.

Kishacoquillas Valley in Mifflin County is over a hundred miles from Lancaster County. Within that one thirty-mile long valley, John A. Hostetler, an authority on the Amish, has documented five Amish groups, three Mennonite groups, and two Mennonite-related groups, each distinguishable from the other by various external symbols: The "Old School" Amish wear no suspenders on their brown trousers, which are laced in the rear to hold them up; the women wear black kerchiefs, because bonnets are taboo. Their buggies have white tops. But the "Old Schoolers" divided into two groups in the early 1940s over the style of a roof. The *Ordnung* of the Old Schoolers prohibits a projecting roof at the gable ends of a building. When a member bought a farm from a non-Amish family, he was told by Church officials to saw off the projecting roof. Not everyone in the congregation agreed, however, and when a member built a doghouse with the prohibited roof style to demonstrate his feelings, the matter brought the group to the breaking point.

Another group, the Byler Amish, also called the "Bean-soupers" (for their custom of serving bean soup after the Sunday preaching even though this practice is also shared by the Old Schoolers), is distinguished by the single suspender on their trousers and the yellow tops on their buggies. Still another group, the Renno Amish, are much like the Amish of Lancaster County with some exceptions: the men, for example, have only one suspender, like the "Bean-soupers." The Zook Amish have two suspenders, shorter hair, zippers on their jackets and—since 1954—automobiles. The Zook Amish are not Old Order Amish, but Beachy Amish, a general term for liberal groups that accept automobiles, electricity, and meeting houses for worship, although they retain many other traditions. Three more Kishacoquillas Valley groups are Mennonite; two additional Protestant groups have among their members people who have left the Amish church.

Hostetler suggests that such breakups actually help to preserve things as they are. Individuals who are dissatisfied leave one district to join another, usually less strict, district. But when there is a group of dissidents, it may be easier to split off and form a new church, keeping much of the old and adopting only the desired changes. The old church stays as it was.

Although exact figures are not available and estimates vary considerably, the Amish population in the United States is thought to be close to 50,000 and still growing. The *Mennonite Yearbook and Directory* of 1975 estimates about 22,500 Old Order Amish members; three-quarters of them in Ohio, Pennsylvania, and Indiana, and the rest scattered among fifteen other states, plus Ontario. The *Yearbook* also counts more than 3,000 "Beachy" Amish, the more liberal automobile-owning branch. These figures, however, refer only to baptized members. Since members are baptized in their late teens, and since the Amish have very large families, that total can be increased by more than one hundred percent. Because of the large families, and despite the fact that many young Amish do drop out of the church, it is a growing population. One set of statistics shows a jump from 25,800 Old Order Amish in 1940 to 33,000 in 1950, to 43,800 in 1960, a rate of increase that has slowed in the past decade. Few of

*Father and son share a ride behind
a quick-stepping horse.* GERALD DODDS

them are converts to the Amish faith, although conversion is not completely unknown. To be Amish is to grow up Amish, indoctrinated at every phase of life by the family, the church, and the community, a difficult process for a convert to duplicate.

Thirty years ago many non-Amish writers and observers were predicting the demise of the Amish culture. The more pessimistic believed that the pressures of the modern world would prove irresistible, and that the Amish would have been absorbed into the mainstream by the 1960s.

They were wrong.

It's true that every society changes to some extent, and the Amish are no exception. And in every society there are a few people who cannot adjust. Many leave. A few retreat into alcoholism, mental illness, and even suicide (the suicide rate among the Amish is about the same, though possibly a little higher, as it is for the country as a whole). And some exert pressure for changes in the *Ordnung* that result in splits.

But the vigorous, God-loving people whose ancestors survived the purges of the sixteenth century seem likely to withstand the pressures of the twentieth. There will probably be handsome Amish boys like Samuel Beiler to be photographed for many years to come.

BELIEF

Sunday Preaching, Daily Living

EARLY SUNDAY morning Sarah Beiler counts the *schnitz* pies one more time: there are three dozen of them, baked on Friday by Sarah and Hannah and Annie and some of the women who live close by. Cut six ways, that's 216 slices, more than enough to feed all the people who will be gathering soon for the preaching service, to be held at their farm this Sunday.

Sarah and her family have spent all the extra time they could squeeze out of their busy days of the past week to get ready for the event. The size of a church district is determined by the number of people who can be accommodated in an individual farmhouse for the Sunday preaching. Houses built by the Old Order Amish are con-

structed with folding doors between the rooms on the
first floor, so that the entire downstairs can be opened up.
But for the Beiler family this is a more complicated
procedure than usual since all the quilts and other kinds
of needlework that Annie has for sale in the living room
had to be packed away. Once that was done, the whole
house was thoroughly cleaned, floors polished, windows
washed, everything made ready. Even Samuel and young
Elam and Amos were pressed into service, although they
made no pretense of feeling that housecleaning was appropriate work for men.

Sarah enjoys the food preparation much more than she
does the cleaning. She and her mother and sister are going
to serve lunch to all the worshippers after the preaching
is over. There are about ninety members in their church
district, but with all the unbaptized people like Sarah and
her brothers, there will be more than 175 mouths to feed.
In some places it is the custom to serve thick bean soup,
but the district to which the Beiler family belongs feels
that the meal should be much simpler, really only a snack
to hold everyone over until they get home to their regular
Sunday dinners. Annie is making pickled beets and eggs,
letting hard-boiled eggs soak in the red juice and spices
to take on both the flavor and the color. There will also
be bread, butter, jam, cottage cheese, and apple butter—
most of the items homemade—as well as Hannah's spe-
cialty, bread-and-butter pickles. And, of course, the pies
made from the dried apple slices that Sarah "schnitzed"
so diligently. Amos reminds them to have plenty of

cookies—molasses cookies are his favorite—to pass to the young children during the long service.

Although taking the Sunday preaching involves a lot of extra effort for the already hardworking Beiler family, it is a day of great significance for them. The preparation becomes, for them on their Sunday, a part of the religious act itself. Most of the labor of clearing out furniture and cleaning the rooms and of baking the innumerable pies and cookies is finished by Friday evening. Although the men help with the heaviest work, most of the burden falls on the women, who enlist the reluctant young boys.

. On Saturday afternoon, after the housecleaning was finished, Ike Riehl arrived with the wagon loaded with benches and the big wooden box of hymnals, all the property—and the only property—of the church district. The men carry in the heavy backless oak benches and arrange them in rows in the kitchen, the living room, and the first-floor bedroom. Not everyone will be able to see the preachers, but they will be able to hear them.

At last everything is ready. The Beiler family is up at five o'clock on Sunday morning as on weekdays, to attend to the routine chores and the last-minute details. By eight o'clock the first buggies are rolling up the lane. Samuel . has been appointed to act as hostler, and the duty falls to him to make sure that the buggies are parked conveniently in an empty field and the horses taken care of with hay and water. He hands each driver a numbered slip of paper so that the owner can later claim the right buggy from the collection of nearly identical vehicles.

Jacob Beiler is on hand to greet the worshippers. Among the first to arrive are the bishop and the other ministers. They shake hands with each other and with Jacob, and with each of the men as they drift in. The women, who have been dropped off in the barnyard, make their way toward the kitchen, while the men and boys greet one another and then gather in little groups under the overhang of the barn, dividing themselves without forethought according to age and marital status. The young, unmarried men seldom cluster with the slightly older married men, who in turn keep apart from the bearded patriarchs.

Toward nine o'clock, one of the ministers comments that it's about time to get started, and the men and boys move toward the house, filing in in traditionally determined order. The bishop and the other ministers go first, followed by the old men of the congregation, the middle-aged men, the young men, and finally the unmarried boys. Meanwhile, Sarah and her sister Hannah come in, Hannah near the front of the line with the baptized young women. Sarah solemnly shakes hands with the minister, as all the others do, and takes her place with the unbaptized girls.

Unlike her brother, Sarah is looking forward to the day when she will be old enough for baptism. She is certain that she will not delay it, as Samuel is doing, that she will be eager and happy to be a member of the church, like her parents. Sarah wants very much to be like her parents, and she is afraid that Samuel does not. What if he refuses to be baptized? What if he leaves the Amish com-

This family buggy has a black top; not all districts permit sliding glass doors. GERALD DODDS

pletely and joins some other group and they never see him
again? What if he gives in to their father and joins, and
then he does something wrong and must be shunned?
Sarah glances at her brother Samuel with his clear, blue
eyes and his wavy brown hair still cut much too close to
his ears. Sarah is very fond of him.

At last everyone has entered the house and found a
seat, women and girls on the benches on one side of the
room, men and boys on the other. The bishop and ministers go to an upstairs bedroom for council. There are always matters that must be talked over before they begin
their participation. As soon as they are gone, one of the
men in the congregation announces a hymn and number
from the *Ausbund*. The men still have their hats on, but
with one gesture they take them off at the announcement
of the hymn and put them on the floor under their
benches. In other church districts, entirely different customs may be observed: in some, the hats are piled outside;
in others, they are hung on hooks instead of placed under
the seats.

Amish singing is unique. There is never any accom-
paniment, and the hymns are sung in unison because
musical instruments and part-singing are forbidden by
the *Ordnung*. The hymn begins, led by the *Vorsänger*,
who sings the first word, using as many as six or more sus-
tained notes, to establish the pitch. The congregation
joins the *Vorsänger* on the second word of the first line,
sung so slowly that it sounds like a chant. Then he sings
the first word of the second line, the congregation joining in, and so on. The role of the *Vorsänger* is a demand-

ing one, requiring a good sense of pitch and as much informal training as necessary to master the difficult tunes. Some experts believe that Amish singing is derived from Gregorian chants of the Middle Ages and observe that the relative slowness of the singing is an indication of the degree of conservatism of the congregation: the more slowly the hymns are sung, the more they resemble a drawnout chant, the less attuned the group is likely to be to the modern world. Scholars who have studied the Amish find that some groups sing four verses of the *Lobelied,* the most widely used Amish hymn, over a period of about twenty minutes, while other more liberal groups sing the same four verses in about half that time. *Lobelied* (*S' Lobg'sang* in dialect) is always sung as the second hymn of the service in every Amish church district.

The words of the hymns are all printed in the *Ausbund,* the oldest Protestant hymnal in use. The *Ausbund* has the German texts of 140 hymns with verses that fill 812 pages, but there are no musical notes for any of them. The tunes themselves have been preserved and passed from generation to generation *solely by ear* for more than two hundred and fifty years and are thought to be based on old popular German songs. The words to these "slow tunes," as they are called, were poems and testimonials written by Anabaptists during their imprisonment, telling of their sorrow and loneliness.

After a few such hymns have been sung, the ministers come down from the second floor and the preaching begins. There are several sermons, primarily in High German, but often with a mixture of Pennsylvania Dutch and

English. The style is singsong; the preacher's voice begins as a kind of unintelligible mutter that gradually
builds to an audible level. As his emotion deepens, the
preacher's voice ascends to a higher and louder pitch,
dropping abruptly at the end of each phrase. Even the
preaching has a chanted quality. The effect is sometimes
soporific. It lasts for a long time—at least three hours—
and even on the uncomfortable backless wooden benches,
some of the worshippers have been known to doze off.

The long Sunday preaching is not an easy time for
young children who must endure the hours of confine-
ment. Katie sits soberly next to her mother on a bench in
the kitchen with the women who have small babies; the
occasional noises they make don't disrupt the others.
Annie can see that Elam and Amos are enduring the
drawnout service, but she guesses they are already thinking about lunch. When she feels that the little ones in
the other rooms with their parents are getting restless, she
quietly carries out a plate of cookies and a glass of water
and starts it unobtrusively at the end of one row. The children help themselves to a cookie and a sip of water, passing the plate and glass up and down the rows until they
need refilling.

At last the service is over. All the members genuflect,
kneeling on both knees, at the benediction, and after the
last hymn everyone files out. The mood changes immediately. A few of the men help to take out some of the
benches and to push others together to form tables. The
women responsible for the food begin to serve in shifts,
starting with the oldest people, ending with the young

boys and girls. After the remains of the meal have been cleared away, the people break into groups, divided traditionally by age and sex, and spend the afternoon in conversation that ranges from serious religious matters to crops and the weather to a coming wedding or a visit from out-of-town relatives or the illness of one of the community. Some of the neighbors are staying for supper, and although most of the food is ready, there is still a lot of work to be done.

Annie is happy to have the company. A friendly, gregarious woman, she is at her best when her house is filled with people and she can feed them well. Her girls are good helpers in the kitchen, and the women visitors pitch in and get things done.

Jacob is a quiet man: he does not enjoy the fuss and visiting as much as Annie does. But he is a capable host, and he has been looking forward to having some time with Joseph Fisher, one of his oldest friends, to talk about Samuel. Joseph Fisher is a preacher. He began his religious role several years ago, without training or preparation, when his name was placed in nomination for deacon, one of the three kinds of minister. He and all the other candidates who had received at least three votes from the congregation filed past a table at the front of the room where the preaching had been held. On the table was a row of Bibles. Each candidate picked up a Bible; inside the one Joseph chose was a slip of paper with a verse on it. There were no slips in the other Bibles, and Joseph knew that the lot had fallen upon him. As deacon, among other responsibilities, he acted as go-between in arranging marriages: it was Joseph who had visited Abe Miller's house to tell them that John Beiler, Jacob's oldest son, wished to marry their daughter. Then, old John Riehl became too sick to keep on in his role as preacher, and Joseph took his place. It is understood that when the bishop dies or becomes too old, Joseph may be chosen to succeed him. The men who assume these roles are generally among the most conservative in the community, nominated because they have shown that they are "model" Amish, successful farmers who observe the *Ordnung* meticulously. Joseph Fisher is such a man.

Puffing cigars while they walk out behind the barn through the orchard, Jacob speaks to his old friend once again about his concern for young Samuel. The preacher sympathizes; his own boy has shown some of the same worldly tendencies. But Samuel is just seventeen, Joseph reminds the worried father. Perhaps he will change in a year's time—most boys are baptized between the ages of eighteen and twenty-two and there is certainly plenty of time. But Jacob and Joseph are not sure which approach is better: to try to talk him into being baptized as soon as possible, knowing that the threat of *Meidung* will force him to mend his ways but could also drive him away altogether; or to leave Samuel alone for another couple of years, hoping that maturity will bring him around to right-thinking, an approach that holds the danger of allowing him to be exposed even longer to the evil temptations of the world. It is a hard problem, they agree. But no decision needs to be made just yet. In another few months they will talk again.

Samuel sees his father and the preacher talking privately, and he guesses that they are talking about him. More and more he thinks about his future, and the thought troubles him. He daydreams about the big bright world out there, apparently beyond his grasp, and he yearns to explore it. Maybe, he thinks to himself, he can join the service. He pictures himself at the controls of a navy aircraft, with a decent haircut and a good-looking uniform and the keys to a car in his pocket. But on the other hand . . . he thinks about Nancy Esch, who will be coming back to the singing that night in the barn, and he thinks about his older brother and about his friends, and he wonders to himself, as he has wondered many, many times, how he can get a taste of the outside world and still come back to this, the only place he really knows, for the kind of life he has been brought up for.

Samuel has, he believes, a few more months until his father will begin to pressure him again. The last group was baptized in September, a month before the fall communion service. Not until May, after the spring communion, will the next class of instruction be organized. Then the applicants will meet with the ministers during the regular preaching service on a half-dozen Sundays to receive an explanation of the *Ordnung* and the scriptures and beliefs basic to Amish life. The young people will be made very much aware that the vows they are taking are for a lifetime.

On the day of the last baptism in his district, Samuel. knowing that his time was coming, paid close attention to all that took place. After the opening hymns had been sung, during which the boys and girls met in the upstairs room with the ministers, they filed in, the girls in black caps and dresses with white organdy capes and aprons, the boys wearing the black *Mutze*. Next came the ministers. When they were seated, the congregation stopped singing and the preaching began. After nearly two hours of sermons, the applicants knelt and each in turn answered the bishop's questions, confessing belief in Jesus Christ, renouncing the devil and the world with all its wicked ways, and promising to keep the *Ordnung*, faithfully and forever.

With the deacon's wife to remove the girls' caps, the bishop laid his hands on the head of each in turn; then the deacon poured water, dipped from a bucket, into the cupped hands of the bishop, who let the water flow onto each head as he baptized in the name of the Father, the Son, and the Holy Spirit. Each new member was then greeted with the holy kiss, an ancient symbol of love and fellowship between believers. After more preaching, hymns, and prayers, the service was over, the rite of passage complete: there could be no turning back.

If Samuel makes up his mind to submit to destiny, he, like every baptized person, will enter wholly into the life of the church, becoming a part of the rhythm and cycle of Amish religious observance. Although each individual's life is inseparably interwoven with religious beliefs, the demands for public performance of worship are relatively few. In most Protestant churches and in the Roman Catholic Church, there is a calendar of prayer and ritual that schedules each day, week, month, and season of the church year. The Amish calendar is much simpler. The two great Sundays of communion, in spring and fall, with the days of preparation and fasting that precede them, are the high points of Amish religious observance.

In between are the preaching services on alternate Sundays. (No one seems to know why the preaching service is held only every other Sunday, instead of every week, but all know that it has always been that way.) On the preaching Sunday before each communion, members endure a day-long service of preparation in which the *Ordnung* is once again brought into sharp focus. Taboos are reviewed and each member must express acceptance of the rules by which they all must live—rules that govern every aspect of life: farming techniques, building styles, dress, home furnishings, transportation, entertainment. Everything. Members must examine their own consciences, confess their faults, promise to correct their mistakes. Unrepentant sinners—those who are known to have broken rules but who stubbornly refuse to admit their errors—are excommunicated and the *Meidung* is invoked.

Just before the communion Sunday, the Amish observe a fast day. Fasting means skipping breakfast and spending the morning in meditation before the fast is broken. Some districts prohibit work on the two yearly fast days. The preparatory service and communion service each occupy the members for a full Sunday. The young, unbaptized Amish are exempt from the ordeal.

The wife at whose home the service is held bakes the bread that is broken for the communion, and wine or grape juice is sipped from a common cup. Then recalling

how Jesus washed the feet of his disciples as an example
of humility, the Amish follow the communion service
with a ceremony of footwashing. Shoes and stockings are
removed. The women in one room and the men in another take turns washing one another's feet in buckets of
water. When they have finished the ritual, each pair of
foot washers embraces and exchanges the holy kiss.

In addition to Sunday services are the great celebra-
tions of the Christian church, observed by the Amish with
total absence of pomp and ceremony: Christmas is passed
quietly with family dinners and the exchange of simple
gifts; no tree, no decorations, no Santa Claus. Good Friday is a day of prayer and fasting, followed by Easter, for
which the children sometimes dye and hide eggs. Ascen-
sion Day, forty days after Easter, and Pentecost or Whit-
sunday on the eleventh Sunday after Easter are Amish
holidays that are anticipated as good excuses for outdoor
recreation, like fishing and hiking and playing ball.
Thanksgiving and New Year's Day are also observed, and
in some communities the day after Christmas and the
Mondays following holidays that fall on Sunday are observed as holidays, too.

Underpinning the *Ordnung,* to which Samuel will have
to agree if and when he becomes a baptized member of the
faith, is a solid foundation of belief that gives structure
and coherence to the seemingly odd and sometimes contradictory customs and practices of the Amish.

One of the most important tenets of the Amish faith is
non-conformity: separation from the world. Non-con-

formity to the Amish does not mean "doing your own thing"; instead, it means refusal to follow standards set by a world they consider inherently evil and is based on Romans 12:2: "Be not conformed to this world: but be ye transformed by the renewing of your mind, that ye may prove what is that good, and acceptable, and perfect, will of God." In practical terms this belief accounts for the distinctive dress and rejection of most modern conveniences which are part of the wicked world.

Because they are separate from the world, are in fact a "chosen people," the Amish believe they must guard against any alliances that would join them with the world. Therefore, they heed the admonition of 2 Corinthians 6:14: "Be ye not unequally yoked together with unbelievers: for what fellowship hath righteousness with unrighteousness? and what communion hath light with darkness?" This yoking with unbelievers has many manifestations that are not apparent to the non-Amish: for instance, having electricity or a telephone is not so much a sign of being "worldly"; after all, it's all right to have a kerosene refrigerator or a one-cylinder gasoline engine in the cellar for pumping water, but an electric line or a telephone line to one's house is a "yoke" with an unbeliever— the power company and the telephone company. Business partnerships with non-Amish are forbidden. And marriage exclusively within the groups is preserved; even marriage with a young person from a different district with a slightly different *Ordnung* is discouraged because of the problem of the more conservative group labeling the more liberal as "unbelievers." Refusal to swear oaths and to hold public office is part of Amish insistence on separateness.

The pacifism and non-resistance practiced by the Amish are based on Jesus' answer to Pilate: "My kingdom is not of this world; if my kingdom were of this world, then would my servants fight, that I should not be delivered to the Jews: but now is my kingdom not from hence." (John 18:36) The Amish refuse to bear arms, but during times of national emergency and war they have been drafted into some form of alternate service. They think of themselves as "defenseless Christians," and when they are confronted with hostility from their non-Amish neighbors or local authorities, they prefer to pull up stakes and move on rather than to stay and defend their rights.

Everything Samuel has experienced as he has been growing up has reinforced his beliefs. It is not that he doubts or questions the validity of these beliefs but that he sits on the fence, wanting the security of the Amish life that he knows so well and also wanting the excitement of the "other" world of which he knows very little. Once baptized, there can be no turning back. He must live with the rules, to the letter of the law. Exceptions are never made and deviations are never tolerated. It's a black-or-white, right-or-wrong philosophy.

In other churches the threat of hell in the next life deters some rule breakers in this life, but the Amish are controlled immediately by the force of the *Meidung,* the shunning. When the pull of "the world" is too strong for some and they are drawn toward its wicked ways—an unapproved farm implement, or too many gadgets on the dashboard of the buggy—the leaders of the church visit

The triangular shawl and prayer cap are traditional garb for Amish women. GERALD DODDS

the errant member. Either he—and it is more likely to be a *he* than a *she*—gives in, and mends his ways, or the *Bann* is invoked—excommunication—and the social pressure of the *Meidung* is brought to bear against him: no one, not even members of his family, including his wife, may have anything to do with him, may conduct business with him, or eat with him or speak to him. The *Meidung* remains in force until the sinner makes the required changes in his life and kneels before the congregation or the ministers, asking forgiveness. It can, and sometimes does, remain in force for a lifetime. But few individuals can resist such pressure for long. There are two ways out: to yield, or to leave the district for a more liberal church. Either way, the wayward one no longer acts as an influence on others in the church.

The Amish are strong believers in life after death; in fact, they regard life on earth as purely temporary, a preparation for eternity. Therefore, an Amish family, enduring the shunning of one of its members, believes that the unrepentant sinner has not only cut himself off from family and church in this lifetime, but forever. To the devout Amish person, eternity has more reality than life on earth.

Samuel, brooding near the barn, sees his father and preacher Joseph returning from their walk, their heads bent, and wonders if they are still talking about him. Samuel is fully aware that the reactions of his parents, if he refuses baptism, or if he accepts it and then breaks a rule, would go far beyond anger or disappointment: they would believe that he is lost to them *forever*. He knows, too, the importance of the commandment to "honor thy father and thy mother"—not only now but for the rest of his life. For even after he is an independent adult, and even after his parents have died and he is himself a grandfather, Samuel will be bound by that commandment to do what he believes his parents would have wished.

"Florida," Sam's cousin Ben has suggested. "That's where I'm going this winter, as soon as the tobacco is done. Why don't you come along, Sam?"

And Sam is tempted. Many young Amish men—as well as their elders—have discovered the pleasure of a winter vacation in Florida. Older adults relax in the sun and return home again, but sometimes the young men, and less frequently the young women, stay in Florida and get jobs, cutting off their long hair and adopting "English" clothes. In the spring, when it's time to plow and plant again, most of them go back to the farm.

Running off to Florida, or to the city, is one of the more extreme activities of restless young men that some Amish parents tolerate, along with owning a car or racing their buggies on the highway or sneaking into movies. Baptism will probably settle all that; marriage certainly will. Youth is a time for getting all the wildness out of one's system, before the responsibilities of marriage and family descend on one's shoulders.

A far greater threat to the Amish is the young person who thinks too much, who begins to question the validity of the beliefs of his religion and to notice the inconsistencies of a lifestyle he is being asked to accept unquestioningly. The Amish know from long experience how to cope with rowdies; the ones who indulge in intellectual activity are far harder to handle.

John Beiler's old friend Aaron Fisher is an example. Sam remembers when all the young people knew that Aaron had a "strange belief." He had stopped smoking, would not join his friends in a forbidden beer, refused to listen to their dirty jokes, and hinted that he had been attending a Bible study group. Suddenly Aaron seemed serious and studious. He stopped all of his running around and began to corner his friends and argue with them. Eventually the elders of the church called on his family. When Aaron refused to change, he was excommunicated and shunned. He soon left the Amish church, moved away from Leacock Township, and joined a fundamental Christian church where his "strange belief" was compatible with the doctrine.

In the house Samuel's mother and sisters are cooking for the friends and neighbors who are staying for supper. Most of the other families have gone home to tend to their chores and visit their relatives and enjoy their own big meals. After the last of the adults has left the Beiler farm, there will be a "singing" in the barn for all the young people of courting age. Everybody will be there, and Samuel knows he'll have a good time, singing and talking and eating the snacks his sisters have fixed, and driving Nancy home afterwards in his buggy.

It's not an easy life, but thinking of Nancy, Sam concludes that it may not be such a bad one.

WORK

Close to the Land, Close to God

JACOB BEILER is expecting a good yield this year. Like many other Amish farmers in Lancaster County, Jacob has planted tobacco as his principal cash crop. He has eight acres of it—all he and his family can manage—and although it requires a lot of work, the rewards are worth it: he anticipates getting around a thousand dollars an acre for it. In 1974 the tobacco crop in Lancaster County amounted to twenty-six million pounds, worth roughly thirteen million dollars to local farmers, a large percentage of whom are Amish.

Jacob remembers when he was a young man, just starting out on his own in the 1950s. In those days, Pennsylvania seed leaf tobacco was raised as the inside wrappers for cigars. (The outer wrappers were shade-grown in Connecticut.) But tobacco companies were introducing a new product that threatened to make the careful hand methods of the Amish farmers virtually obsolete. Small and imperfect leaves that were once good only for filler would instead be ground up fine, combined with a binding agent, and rolled out in uniform sheets that would be cut into wrappers. With the availability of such a cheap substitute, the high-grade hand-picked leaves of Lancaster County tobacco would no longer command premium prices. Although in the 1970s the homogenization process has been adopted to a certain extent, it is the competition from foreign markets that has created the greatest change. Today most cigar wrappers are imported, and the tobacco grown in Lancaster County is used for chewing tobacco.

Raising tobacco involves every member of Jacob's family nearly every month of the year. Tobacco requires more man-hours of hand labor than practically any other farm product. Although the end result is different than it was a generation or so ago, the methods remain unchanged.

Jacob has hardly delivered the seventy-pound bales to the tobacco company in January than the cycle begins again. During the growing season he allowed some of the prime stalks to go to seed; these seeds are put in jars for sprouting. Meanwhile, as soon as the ground has thawed, in late February or early March, Jacob and Samuel begin plowing the fields and preparing the seed beds. Before the sprouted seeds are planted in April, Jacob hires a man with a gasoline-operated steamer or old-fashioned steam engine to sterilize the soil, killing the weeds that would crowd out the seedlings before they are established. Annie and the girls plant the seeds in the prepared beds, raking the seeds into the finely pulverized earth and covering the surface with thin muslin.

Beginning in May and continuing through June at regular intervals, the women pull the tender seedlings from the seed beds and arrange them in shallow wooden boxes. While Jacob or Samuel guides the team through the fields, Elam and Amos sit on the back of the tobacco planter with the boxes of seedlings, dropping a seedling into the hole punched and watered by the contraption on which they're riding. A few days after the planting, the children go through the fields again, replacing plants sliced off by cutworms.

In early July it's time to begin hoeing. All eight acres must be thoroughly hoed, a job that keeps all of the Beiler family in the fields until it's too dark to see. Next, each plant must be topped—the top cut off so that the energy of the plant goes into growing broad leaves rather than a tall stalk—and chemically treated to inhibit the growth of suckers, or new shoots. The use of the chemical is probably the one recent innovation in tobacco farming in Pennsylvania.

In August, Jacob begins to cut the first of the mature tobacco plants, slicing the tough stalks a few inches above the ground and spearing the end of each stalk with a wooden lath. The laths, a half-dozen stalks on each, are taken by wagon to the tobacco barn where they are hung

*Plowing by hand keeps a young farmer
close to the soil.* GERALD DODDS

on scaffolding. By the time the entire crop has matured and been cut, the barn is filled from floor to ceiling with laths of tobacco. Vertical slats on the side of the barn are propped open to allow circulation of air. By late November the tobacco has dried and the curing is completed. Jacob and the boys take the rich brown tobacco stalks off the laths and store them in the cellar. In December the family begins stripping, removing the leaves from the stalks one at a time, a process that has not yet been automated. Then the leaves are sorted and baled.

After the stripping is finished, representatives of the several tobacco companies in Lancaster visit the tobacco farmers, inspect the bales of tobacco, and make their offers. Jacob must either accept or reject the offer, knowing that if he sells too quickly another agent might come along and offer more but aware that, if he holds out too long, other offers might be lower. Misjudgment may cost him hundreds of dollars. Annie and the children know that on the days of the bidding Jacob's temper seems to be quite short.

The Amish are required by doctrine to be farmers or to work in farm-related occupations. Working the soil keeps one close to God; hard physical labor is good in itself. Farming helps to hold the family together, living and working as a unit in a way that would not be possible if the members worked away from home. And it keeps the temptations of the world at bay.

Farming as a tenet of the Amish faith dates back to the early years of the Anabaptists in Europe. Traditionally, most Anabaptists were farmers by choice. But they were also refugees, subjected to discrimination and denied the right to own land. They became tenant farmers, on the bottom of the social pyramid and forced to make do with the poorest land available. In order to eke a living from the land, they had to be both hardworking and innovative in their methods.

When the first Amish arrived in Pennsylvania, they were pleased to find black walnut trees that meant fertile land and blue stones streaked with white that indicated limestone soil. They took over land that had been abandoned by less diligent farmers who thought it easier to clear new land as the old soil wore out. The Amish knew well the importance of crop rotation, planting several crops in succession to preserve and improve soil fertility. Clover, for example, restored nitrogen to the soil depleted by other crops and made excellent feed for cattle, which then produced manure, in turn extremely important for the soil.

The Amish were barn builders as well as soil builders. An old saying among the non-Amish contends that when an Amish person buys land, he is more likely to build a barn on it than a house. While "English" farmers let their animals roam and provided rather flimsy shelter for them, the Amish introduced stall feeding. This gave them more land for planting, and manure accumulated where it could be easily collected and used.

The Amish and the Mennonites are responsible for the introduction of the Swiss bank barn, built on two levels with a ramp so that a hay wagon could be driven directly to the upper story. One observer noted that Amish barns were as large as palaces, while the families dwelled in simple homes—the sure sign of a good farmer.

As a result of their hard work and innovative techniques, the Amish soon transformed the area they settled in eastern Lancaster County into what an early journalist called the "Garden Spot of Pennsylvania" and almost invariably prospered better than their "English" neighbors. For many years the Amish maintained their reputation as outstanding farmers, even as the non-Amish began to mechanize their operations. But mechanization requires increased acreage in order to produce enough to support the cost of the machinery. The size of non-Amish farms grew and so did the overhead, but net profit did not. What the Amish understood is that use of modern farm equipment does not increase acreage yield; it cuts down the number of hours the farmer and his family must spend in the field. The general trend in the nation has been to increasingly larger farms, increasingly mechanized. For the large commercial farmers, it is an endless cycle: the more land, the more machinery needed, the more expense, the bigger crops needed to generate more money, the more land required, and so on, around and around. Amish farms, meanwhile, have remained the same: fifty acres is about average. In fact, because of the population increase and the scarcity of good farm land, Amish farms tend to be smaller than they once were.

Everything the Amish know about farming has been passed along orally from father to son for generations. Furthermore, they want nothing to do with "book farming," even when such knowledge would not be incompatible with their beliefs. Their lack of education and technical expertise is a handicap, but they continue to overcome these drawbacks with extra care, extra effort, and extra time.

Although tobacco is Jacob's main cash crop, it is by no means the limit of his farming. But it does make the cycle of his year different from that of the Amish farmer in other areas where tobacco is not grown. He feeds steers for market and buys chickens to produce eggs. He and Samuel and a hired hand seed clover and alfalfa, rotating it with fields of corn, oats, and wheat, together with potatoes and minor cash crops, such as peas and tomatoes. In addition, the family tends a large garden to produce food for its own use.

Amish desire to remain separate from the world and refusal to be "yoked with an unbeliever" is manifested in avoidance of anything involving the government. Although the Amish pay taxes, like everyone else, they will not accept any subsidies from the government. When overproduction threatens the farm prices, Amish farmers voluntarily cut back on production of their cash crops, but they will not accept subsidies for milk, for instance, or for not growing a crop on a piece of land, explaining that they cannot take money for work they have not done.

Samuel Beiler is sick of raising tobacco. When he has a farm of his own, he promises himself, it will be a dairy farm. He dislikes hoeing tobacco under the hot July sun; cutting and spearing the tobacco and hoisting the laths onto the rafters at the top of the barn are not much easier. But hand-stripping is worst of all. When they are working hour after hour under the gas lamp in the cellar, it seems to Samuel that all he can taste for days is tobacco in the back of his throat. It is a different taste than smoking, which he and his friends all do. Most of the Amish have no particular stand for or against smoking, although none of the women smoke and the men usually stick to cigars. Smoking is disapproved in some districts, but they are likely to be where tobacco is not a principal source of income.

Although Amish farmers have had to make almost no changes in their ways of producing tobacco for market, those who are involved in dairy farming have encountered many problems. Dairying is a highly mechanized industry, and the milk companies adhere to strict standards, established by law, that cannot be bent.

But the Amish are ingenious in observing the letter of the *Ordnung*. Electricity-by-wire is taboo (the "yoke with the unbeliever"); electricity-by-generator is acceptable. Therefore, diesel generators power the automatic milking machines, coolers, electric lights, and all the other equipment required for efficient, high-standard operation of a dairy farm.

One problem was harder to solve. The Amish will not do business on a Sunday (even the self-service roadside stands set up by the Amish housewives as an outlet for their eggs are locked on Sundays). Pickups by the milk processors, whose totally automated plants run continuously, were scheduled for Sunday, like any other day, and the Amish farmers balked. When the milk companies refused to make concessions, it seemed that many Old Order Amish had lost their market for fluid milk.

The Amish answer was to establish a cheese factory. In the early days of the American colonies, cheese making was carried on at home by industrious housewives; in the mid-nineteenth century, cheese making was moved from the farm to the factory. It is one of the few industries well-suited to the Amish way of doing things. Amish farmers unable or unwilling to afford the expense of converting their farms to meet the rigid specifications of the milk companies found a satisfactory market for their fresh milk.

Amish ingenuity, based on literal-mindedness and a knack for making do, is again demonstrated in the solution to a small but important problem that confronted the owners of the cheese factory. Their business required a telephone; although the Amish are allowed to *use* a telephone, they are not permitted to *have* one (the "yoke" again). The solution was to have the company install an outdoor phone booth with a public pay telephone and a loud bell on non-Amish property next door to the cheese factory.

Samuel dreams of a dairy farm, and he may one day have it. But he will have to work hard to attain that goal. Setting up a young farmer with a farm of his own is a costly procedure.

One of the main goals of every Amish father is to save up enough money so that he will be able to provide a farm for each of his sons. Lancaster County, about an hour's drive from Philadelphia, is in one of the nation's most thickly settled urban areas, the corridor running from Boston to Washington. There is great pressure for land, and this has caused the price of acreage to soar. For years the practice was for the Amish to buy the farms of the "English" who were selling their farms and moving to the city or taking non-farming jobs. (They were also a good source of the old-fashioned farming equipment used by the Amish, now so scarce it has nearly attained the status—and the prices—of antiques.) But soon most of the available land had been bought up. Land developers, offering higher prices than Amish farmers can muster, are moving in. Because the Amish have enjoyed a substantial population growth as a result of their large families, they now occupy most of the farming land in the center of the settlement, and they are being forced to buy up land farther away. This places a strain on family ties, but it can't be helped.

Meanwhile, the Lancaster County Amish, with their lucrative tobacco and dairy farming, are among the most prosperous Amish in the nation. Their barns and houses reflect their general well-being. But it is not generally so in Amish settlements in other parts of the country, where the Amish have difficulty in competing with highly mechanized "agribusiness."

Young people who have finished eighth grade and are not needed full time on the farm go out to work. Their salary is turned over to the parents, who save it for investment in livestock and farm machinery when the time comes. Often the boy's first job is as a laborer or a farm

Creak of leather, clank of iron, and soft thud of horses'
hoofs are pleasant sounds to work by. MICHAEL RAMSEY

hand. Later, after he has married, he becomes a tenant farmer, based on the old sharecropping system: he works on another farmer's land and gets a share of the cash crop. While he is still relatively inexperienced, his share may be a third; later it becomes a half. When he is able, he rents the land, often from relatives, and the full profit, after he has paid the rent, is his. The final stage is to have a farm of his own. Until his children are old enough to help him, he will have to hire labor, boys just starting out on the bottom rung of the ladder he himself has just climbed.

Hannah Beiler, wrapped in her shawl against the early morning chill, waits at the end of the lane. Every morning at seven o'clock Mr. Hummer arrives in his battered station wagon to collect her and four other young Amish women from neighboring farms and to drive them to his greenhouse, where they will spend the day preparing special arrangements for local customers and getting ready the plants and fresh flowers that will be sold Tuesday and Friday mornings at the Central Market in Lancaster.

Mr. Hummer is a Mennonite, and he understands more than most of the other "English" what it means to be Amish. Their fundamental beliefs are similar, but the Mennonites accept modern technology and higher education. So although Mr. Hummer's grown children have all gone to college, they have refused military service; Mrs. Hummer wears the cap and the *Holsz duuch* as she drives to the supermarket and works around her modern kitchen.

A generation ago girls of Hannah's age would probably

not have gone to work outside of the home, at least not in the non-Amish community. But the situation has changed. Economic survival of the Amish family still depends on having a large number of children, as it always has. But now the older children often must go out and work to help supplement the farm income.

Although farming was once the only occupation allowed the Amish father, that too has changed. It is no longer always possible for the Amish family to survive by farming alone. Farming still has the highest status, but many Amish men are involved in farm-related businesses: blacksmiths, carriage builders, harness makers, carpenters, furniture makers, butchers. They find work in feed mills, sawmills, dairies, and cheese factories. General factory work has traditionally been prohibited, but in recent years some church districts have relaxed that rule, too. There is more latitude among jobs that young people may accept. But workers of every age are restricted by the limitations of an eighth-grade education.

Hannah enjoys her work. She has always been especially fond of flowers, and she dreams of the day when she will have a home of her own. She has ambitions to grow flowers for sale to tourists, the way her mother sells the quilts. While she works, Hannah's mind often strays to thoughts of Reuben Stoltzfus. Reuben, who has been courting her for nearly three years, works as a carpenter's helper. No one except their parents knows it yet, but they plan to marry in November. In the spring they will move in with Reuben's parents and work as tenants. Hannah will quit her job and take on the fulltime job of

farmer's wife. This is the role that Hannah has been preparing for since childhood, and she looks forward to it. It
has never occurred to her that her life might be any other
way.

There is no question of "liberation" for the Amish
woman. The role of husband and wife are carefully dif-
ferentiated by tradition: the man is in charge of the farming and the woman is in charge of running the household.
They are partners in a business that demands all of their
efforts. Although they do help each other, it seems that
the woman does more work in the fields—hoeing tobacco,
for instance—than the man does in the house. The large
garden is primarily her responsibility, and preserving the
food grown there is her job.

Like the rest of the family, Annie Beiler has very little
"free time." Although the work of the farmer is gov-
erned by the season and influenced by the weather, the
work of the farmer's wife is scheduled by the day—washing on Monday, ironing on Tuesday, baking on Friday,
housecleaning on Saturday, as in the old rhyme. In addition to her household chores, she often operates her own
little business. Many Amish wives hang signs at the end
of the lane for fresh eggs or jellies or noodles. Annie
Beiler, with her flourishing quilt business, is rather un-
usual.

Annie is the first one out of bed in the morning, arising
shortly after half-past four and rousing the rest of the
family. After the milking and barn chores have been completed, the family gathers in the kitchen for a big break-

fast. She has dinner (as the noon meal is called in the country) ready before noon and supper on the table late in the afternoon. After supper she helps with the evening chores and often works in the field with the men until dark. She and the family go to bed early; obviously anyone who needs eight hours of sleep must be in bed by half-past eight when morning comes at half-past four.

If Jacob's hours in the field are made longer than the non-Amish farmers by the necessity of using horses rather than tractor-power, then the same is true of Annie in her household chores without modern mechanical aids. Although there is a gasoline engine in Annie's cellar to pump water, many Amish families still rely on windmills or water power. A creek that runs through a farm can also pump water; the running creek turns a small waterwheel connected to a triangular metal frame that it rocks back and forth. The frame is hitched to a wire that is strung along short poles all the way to the house and barn, sometimes for several hundred yards, where the wire is attached to a pump handle. The pump operates continuously, and the overflow is drained off to the barnyard. It's a simple device, and it works.

Annie has a washing machine that runs by gasoline, too; her refrigerator is also gasoline powered. Her stove burns kerosene; she would prefer bottled gas, but that, too, is forbidden by the *Ordnung* of her district. In the winter, when darkness comes early and there is no work in the fields, Annie spends the evening at the treadle sewing machine, piecing the quilts by the light of a gasoline lamp that provides a bright and steady light.

Annie is an efficient housekeeper, but the simple requirements of the Amish home help to keep chores to a
minimum. There is no wall-to-wall carpeting to be vacuumed; plain, unpatterned linoleum covers the floor.
There are no curtains to wash or draperies to be cleaned;
in Annie's church district only dark green roller shades
are permitted, although some allow plain curtains on the
lower half of the windows. There are no slipcovers to
launder or upholstery to shampoo, because upholstered
furniture is not allowed.

Because Annie, like all other Amish women, has no
other options, and because her work is necessary and
valued, she is basically a contented housewife. No career
beckons her away from the farm and out into the world.
She wishes good husbands for her daughters and good
wives for her sons, knowing that they will, when the time
comes, marry within the group, just as she did. Annie
does not worry about her children, except for Samuel. He
is a good boy, even though he has ideas of which she and
his father do not approve. Jacob seems to feel that if only
Samuel would agree to be baptized, the temptations
would be removed and the problems solved. But Annie
knows better: if Samuel meets the right girl—and maybe
he already has—marriage is what will ultimately settle him
down.

And Annie, like all other Amish women, virtually without exception, is a good model for her daughters. Hannah likes her work at the greenhouse, but she knows that
running her own household someday will be much more
satisfying. She is a good cook and a good manager, both

learned from her mother. She knows that she is strong and capable of working hard beside her husband when he needs her. She loves children, and she believes that she will know exactly what to do to bring them up right. But she wishes very much that her younger brother Samuel, who is such a worry to the family, felt about his future the way she does about hers. She cannot for the life of her understand why he would want it to be any other way.

CUSTOMS

Courtship, Marriage, Life, Death

J ONAS, Samuel's horse, has been groomed to perfect sleekness and hitched to the immaculately polished buggy. The night is clear, and the horse's breath hangs in white puffs in the frosty air; Sarah and Hannah, sharing the seat with Samuel, pull the heavy robe tight across their laps. Samuel, wearing his best suit, sets Jonas trotting briskly toward Ezra King's for the Sunday night singing. The pains he has taken with the buggy, the horse, and his own appearance are not for the benefit of his sisters. For although it is usual for a young man of courting age to drive a sister to the singing, it is the custom to drive another *Maydel* home. And Samuel has made these preparations to please the eye of Nancy Esch.

From the time they reach the age of *Rum Schpringe*—
"running around"—at about sixteen for boys, a little
younger for girls, and for the next half-dozen years until
they marry, Amish teen-agers do much of their socializing
at the singings, usually held at the farm where the preaching service took place in the morning. Although the principal activity is singing hymns, these occasions are more
social than religious. Still they are functions of the church
district, and this helps to keep dating and eventually marriage within the group.

In Lancaster County, young people from several church
districts who are in agreement on points of the *Ordnung*
may get together for a joint singing. Sometimes, rather
than waiting to get to the singing to find a partner for the
evening, they congregate in one of the villages and pair
off first.

In *Amish Society,* John A. Hostetler reports that in
large Amish settlements like Lancaster County which have
many young people and where distances are great, there
is no longer one single group of teen-agers but a number
of gangs, some more conservative than others in beliefs,
practices, and standards of behavior. The Groffies, for
instance, named for the village of Groffdale, are most
liberal: their hair is shorter, their dress more worldly, and
they sneak off to movies and have drivers' licenses and
often own cars. The Ammies, who are generally middle-
of-the-road conservative, have produced many splinter
groups. According to Dr. Hostetler, the Trailers are most
orthodox, and their singings match the traditional descriptions of these events. In liberal gangs, the old-fash-

ioned singings generally turn quickly into rowdy, foot-stomping hoedowns.

The Amish are reluctant to talk about their customs of courtship and marriage, insisting that what goes on in their private lives is no business of the world's. Few "English" attend Amish social activities—a singing, for instance, or a barn dance. "Outsiders are not welcome at these affairs," Hostetler quotes one young man as saying. "They do not want tourists or inquisitors who want to know more about the Amish—but people their own age from town, who come to play and have a good time, that is all right."

The singing to which Samuel, Hannah, and Sarah are going is conservative rather than liberal. A long table has been set up in Ezra's barn; the boys sit down on one side of the table, the girls on the other. In between joking and teasing on both sides of the table, they take turns in the role of *Vorsänger,* calling out the number of the hymn and starting the first word. The hymns used are the "fast tunes," some of them familiar Protestant hymns, rather than the "slow tunes" or chants sung at the preaching service. Around ten o'clock the singing ends, the girls serve snacks, and the couples, now paired off, start home. Hannah is with Reuben, as always; Samuel has invited Nancy and has been accepted; Sarah, Samuel is relieved to see, is with Crist Byler. And that, according to traditional accounts, is the end of the evening.

But not always. Sometimes someone produces a harmonica, the table is pushed aside, and the sedate singing turns into a lively barn dance. When "wilder" groups bring out guitars and other forbidden instruments, and the older boys haul in cases of beer, the relatively tame barn dance escalates into a hoedown, and the beards of the Amish fathers wag in dismay at the excesses of modern youth. One problem most Amish parents don't have to worry about: the horse always knows the way home, no matter how much beer the driver has consumed.

The popular image of the Amish as sober, straight-laced, God-fearing people who divide their time between work and worship and who seem to make things difficult for themselves on both counts is essentially correct. But the Amish are also sociable people who like to have a good time among themselves. What they consider an appropriate "good time" changes radically after marriage; before that sobering event the young people are permitted considerable leniency. While the "outside" generally receives the impression that the social life of an Amish teen-ager begins with a singing and ends with a buggy ride home under the stars at a respectably early hour, the fact is that Amish dating is considerably livelier. A non-Amish photographer who managed to get both himself and his camera into a barn dance came out with a picture that shows demure Amish maidens in white head coverings, smoking cigarettes and dancing in the arms of their partners.

On the Saturday night before the "off Sunday"—the alternate weekend when there is no preaching—the young unmarried Amish people conduct their courting. The keynote is secrecy: no matter how long a boy and girl go together before they marry, they are never seen together publicly as a couple, except as they leave a singing or a barn dance. And they never admit their feelings to family or friends, who would tease them mercilessly.

According to tradition, Samuel, who has taken Nancy home from singing several times and has decided that he wants to go a step further, dresses carefully in his best clothes on Saturday evening and announces as casually as possible that he is meeting some of his friends in town. His family carefully refrains from comment, although Amos and Elam giggle to themselves. Annie and Jacob, like all Amish, hold marriage in high esteem. They both know that Samuel's life will change dramatically once he is safely married, and they're perfectly willing to do their part by professing ignorance.

When Samuel is sure that Nancy's parents have gone to bed, Samuel shines his flashlight up at her window. In the days before flashlights he would have tossed a handful of pebbles or dried corn. While he waits in the cold for Nancy to come downstairs and open the door, Samuel wonders to himself whether Nancy will lead him quietly up to her room to spend the night in her bed—talking, with all their clothes on.

"Bundling" is an English word that has no equivalent in Amish dialect, yet the practice of courting in bed fully clothed is usually attributed to the Amish. Historically, however, bundling dates back to New England, and it had more to do with keeping warm in a cold house than it did with sex. The New England Puritans adopted central heating and forsook bundling, but no one is quite sure whether the Amish still do or don't. Apparently bundling has fallen into disfavor in some areas; in other places it is retained as a matter of course. Some ministers condemn the practice, others defend it. It seems that it is the girl's parents, rather than the local *Ordnung,* who have the final say, and progressive Amish are more likely to say no than their more traditional brethren.

There is a saying that if a boy can persuade his girl to take off her prayer cap, she'll have sex with him. Evidently that doesn't happen often, because the rate of pre-marital pregnancies among the Amish in the 1950s, 4.1 percent, was about half the national average, and nearly the same as it had been half a century earlier.

Pre-marital sex is forbidden by the Amish, birth control is taboo, and sex education is non-existent. An unmarried couple accused of having sex is subjected to the *Bann* and the *Meidung* for several weeks. After they have made a full confession before the entire church membership, they are pardoned and readmitted to fellowship. If the girl is pregnant, there is a hasty wedding but none of the disgrace that is attached to forced marriages in the outside world.

One of the persistent myths about the Amish is their inordinate interest in sex, based on the belief that without radio or television or movies there isn't very much else to do in the evening for entertainment. It has even been suggested that the town of Cross Keys, a few miles east of Lancaster, was renamed Intercourse by the sex-obsessed Amish, who probably never use such a Latinism. (The real reason for the change does seem to be lost, however.)

The Amish child growing up on a farm cannot remain totally ignorant of the reproductive processes. The human "facts of life" are not usually assembled until the age of marriage, and it can be assumed that most brides and many of the bridegrooms are still clumsily ignorant of the details on their wedding night.

Hannah has not told anyone except her parents that she and Reuben are planning to marry soon. Annie and Jacob were not surprised at the news. They knew, even though they pretended otherwise, that Reuben had been calling regularly on Hannah, so the question had not been "who" but "when." They have known Reuben Stoltzfus and his family all their lives. For the nearly four years of their courtship, Hannah and Reuben have ridden home from singings, sat by the hour in the chilly kitchen (Jacob had made it clear, through his wife, that there was to be no bundling), attended corn huskings and taffy pulls and, lately, the weddings of their friends, being careful all the time to preserve a veil of secrecy.

Friends and relatives will not know of Hannah's and Reuben's plans to marry until the couple is "published" at the preaching two Sundays before the wedding. Like most Amish weddings, it will be held in November, when the harvest is over but it is not yet time to begin stripping tobacco; December is the second most popular month. And there are traditionally only two possible days in the week that Hannah can consider for her wedding day: Thursday is the first choice and Tuesday is second.

They have decided tentatively on the second Thursday

in November. It is then Reuben's duty to go to the deacon of the church and to ask him to be his *Schteckleimann,* or go-between. Courtship ritual is formalized, but the Amish man is spared the duty of having to ask a stern father for his daughter's hand in marriage; the *Schtecklei- mann* takes care of that. The deacon stops to visit Jacob one evening after the chores are finished, and the two confer. There is not much to be said: Hannah is a hard-working young woman, and he is pleased that she has chosen such a sober, industrious man as Reuben. His mind wanders again to his son Samuel; the right girl might do wonders for him. But he is only seventeen, too young to marry.

Hannah is twenty years old and Reuben is twenty-two. Amish men are usually between twenty-two and twenty-four when they marry, the women between twenty and twenty-two. Although early marriage is associated with large families and a ban on birth control, the average age of Amish couples has been increasing because of the problems of accumulating enough money to establish a household and to acquire land. Reuben, however, is fortunate: he is the youngest of his family, and his father is ready to let him take over the farm.

It is the custom for Amish parents to retire while they are still relatively young, especially if they have a son who needs a farm. For the first few years, until the babies start to come and while Reuben's sister Mattie is still at home, Reuben and Hannah will live in the *Groeszdawdi Haus,* grandfather's house, a section of the farmhouse built to accommodate a second generation. Later when the family has increased and when Reuben has assumed full responsibility for the farm, he and Hannah and their children will move into the larger part of the house, and his parents will go to live in the *Groeszdawdi Haus.*

Since Mattie is twenty-five years old and not yet married, it is almost assumed that she will remain a spinster and continue to live with her parents. There is generally a shortage of young men in the Amish community, because most of the dissidents who leave are male, resulting in an unbalanced population. The remaining men of Mattie's age group have already married. But Reuben hopes that his sister will have a chance to marry at some point. Marriage is important, and widowers, especially younger ones with children still at home, usually remarry. There is in the community a young man whose wife died two years ago. Reuben hopes that he will marry Mattie.

In any case, Reuben is in an enviable position: his father's farm is large and prosperous; Ike Z. Stoltzfus is considered by the other Amish one of the best farmers in the area, and the property is choice. There is not an Amish father in the district who would not be pleased to have his daughter marry Ike Z.'s youngest son.

Jacob nods his approval to the deacon, who reports back to the bishop that the father has given his consent. At the next Sunday preaching, among the other announcements at the end of the service, Reuben and Hannah are "published." According to custom, Hannah is not present. Reuben is there, though, and as soon as the announcement has been made, just before the last hymn is sung, he hitches his horse and buggy and drives to Hannah's house to tell her the news.

The next few weeks, between the announcement and the wedding day, are very busy ones for the Beiler family. There are many preparations to be made, for although the numbers are about the same as for the lunch after the Sunday preaching—over two hundred people will be invited—the food is much more elaborate. This is a time for Jacob to show what a good provider he is. Reuben moves into the Beiler house to assist with the preparations. Hannah sees little of him, though; there is too much to do. His first job is to invite personally the wedding guests, the formidable task of calling on about seventy-five families. All of the invitations are verbal; nothing is written.

An Amish marriage is a very practical affair. Divorce is unknown; separation is rare. The Amish are much more realistic about the expectations of marriage than are the "other" Americans. They do not marry for "love" or "romance" but out of mutual respect and the need for a partner in the kind of life they are expected to live: the farmer needs a wife, and they both need children. Marriage is important to the Amish community. It is a sign that the young people have truly joined the group, the climax of the rite of passage that began with baptism, the signal of the arrival of adulthood and sober responsibility. Unmarried baptized persons, no matter what their age, don't have the status of married people. Marriage provides additional bonds and helps hold the group together. The way the couple feels about each other is less important than the need to establish ties and assume responsibilities.

Although there may have been plenty of hand holding and kissing during the couple's courting days, such affection was always shown in private, and it is assumed that all signs of affection will be kept private during the engagement and after marriage. Any public demonstration would be regarded with distaste.

On the day before Hannah's wedding a dozen couples, Jacob's and Annie's friends and favorite relatives, come to help with the formidable job of preparing the wedding dinner. An Amish wedding is an occasion of solemn ceremony followed by celebration and feasting, certainly the most festive event observed in the community. One of the dishes served will be chicken; by tradition, it is Reuben's duty to cut the heads off the chickens. Preparations begin early in the morning. By the end of the day, dozens of chickens and one fine turkey are stuffed and ready for roasting. Annie doesn't have that kind of capacity in her stove, so the neighbors will take some home to roast in their kitchen and outdoor ovens.

Early on the morning of the wedding day, Reuben and Hannah drive to a neighboring farm where the furniture has been moved out of the house and the wooden benches moved in, as for a Sunday preaching service. It's scarcely daylight when Hannah and Reuben and the two couples who are their attendants arrive at the farm. By half-past nine the field is crowded with carriages belonging to their friends and relatives, and the service begins. The ministers retire to the upstairs council room, just as on preaching Sundays, and the bride and groom follow them. While the guests downstairs sing wedding hymns, the ministers solemnly instruct Reuben and Hannah on their duties as husband and wife.

After the instruction, the ministers and the couple come downstairs again and take their seats at the front of the main room, Reuben and the two men who are his attendants facing Hannah and the two women who are hers. Hannah is not dressed as a bride; she wears no veil, carries no flowers, and will be given no wedding ring. Her dark blue dress is new, but it is exactly like any dress she would wear to a Sunday preaching. With it, Hannah wears a black cap and white shawl and apron.

The sermon is a long one, based on Old Testament passages about marriage, and it is nearly noon when the actual wedding ceremony begins. The questions asked, the answers given, and the vows made, without the aid of a book, are similar to those repeated by couples of other Protestant churches. The ceremony ends when Reuben takes Hannah's right hand and the bishop places his hand on theirs and pronounces a blessing. Reuben and Hannah are husband and wife.

Although the service is not yet over, some of the cooks for the wedding dinner leave quietly to return to the Beiler farm to make sure everything is ready. After the closing prayers and hymn, Hannah and Reuben and their attendants are met by hostlers with buggies, who drive them to the farm. Hannah keeps her eyes cast down. The occasion is serious, and the mood is still solemn.

Meanwhile, the long tables arranged in the living room and kitchen and first floor bedroom are loaded with food: not only the roast chickens but platters of ham and an endless array of side dishes.

The amount of food served and consumed is prodigious. Although there is no grand wedding cake with miniature plastic bride and groom on top, there are on each table several homemade cakes brought by friends, in addition to cookies, bowls of fruit, nuts, and candies.

Hannah and Reuben are seated at the *Eck,* or bridal corner, a table set up in the corner of the living room where they can be seen by the wedding guests who come to take their places, directed to their seats by Jacob, the women on one side of the tables, their backs to the wall, and the men facing them. The cooks have already eaten and are ready to serve. The young unmarried people are at tables in the living room; the older married couples eat in the other rooms. Reuben's old friend John is the *Schnitzer,* the carver, who slices the magnificent turkey that has been brought to the *Eck,* and makes sure that the plates of the bride and groom are kept well filled with the choicest morsels from all the dishes.

After all the seats are taken, the guests bow their heads for a silent blessing on the food. Then Jacob says, in the manner of every Amish host to his guests. "Now you must all reach and help yourselves." And without ceremony, they do.

As soon as the first group has eaten and left the table, their places are taken by the second group. Meanwhile, there is a scramble to wash the dirty dishes and get them back on the table for the second sitting, and the third, and however many more are needed to make sure all the guests have been well fed. Hannah and Reuben stay at the *Eck,* occasionally getting up and mingling with their friends.

After nearly everyone has eaten, the guests, who have brought their own songbooks with them, begin the singing, starting with three wedding hymns that are always sung in the same order, and then moving on to the "fast tunes," with the women as well as the men calling out the tunes and acting as *Vorsänger.* Hannah and Reuben do not join in, restrained by custom from singing at their own wedding so as not to invite bad luck. Late in the afternoon the guests begin to leave, especially those who have some distance to travel and chores to do.

But most of the young people stay on, and eventually supper is served. There is more of everything, including the singing, which finally ends with a semi-religious song that does not appear in the book but is traditionally sung last at Amish weddings. By then everyone is paired off, not always quite willingly in the case of the young boys who are forced by older men to take partners anyway. Still in high spirits, the guests go out to Jacob's barn and play games like "Skip to My Lou." Reuben and Hannah join in for the last time, because as serious married people whose carefree youth is now behind them they will no longer be free to attend singings and barn dances. By midnight nearly everyone has started home; Friday is a work day that begins again for all of them at five o'clock.

It may be worth noting here that Reuben was not tossed over the fence. According to some, the young unbearded men catch the bridegroom and toss him over the barn-yard fence into the arms of the bearded married men—the kind of custom that really should exist, even if it doesn't.

There is no honeymoon for Reuben and Hannah in the worldly sense of the word, but on the weekend after the wedding they begin a long period of visiting relatives around the countryside, getting acquainted with one another's large families, sometimes having lunch with one, supper with another, staying overnight with still a third relative. Along the way they are presented with wedding gifts by people who did not bring them to the wedding. The gifts are usually practical things—kitchen equipment and farm tools, for instance, and homemade presents like table cloths. These gifts, added to the things they have been accumulating on their own during the months and even years before the wedding, help them to equip their own home.

Like many newly married Amish couples, Reuben and Hannah will not live together until the following spring, when their home will be ready. During the winter they continue to spend the work week apart, at the homes of their respective parents, staying together on weekends at the homes of the relatives they are visiting.

The winter passes, the snow melts, the brown earth is

ready for plowing, and at last the *Groeszdawdi Haus* has been fixed up and painted for its new occupants. Samuel helps Reuben carry the furniture, much of it provided by Jacob and Annie, into the house; Sarah and Hannah spread the secondhand bed with one of the handsomest quilts in Lancaster County, stitched with Annie's help during the long winter evenings. While the men carry and the young women arrange and put away, Annie and Reuben's mother, Frances, cook dinner. After they all sit down and ask the silent blessing, Reuben, his new beard already thickly covering his chin, says to the family around his table, "Now you must all reach and help yourselves."

Soon after this, John Beiler, Samuel's older brother, clatters up the lane in his buggy, the flanks of his horse heaving. John hails Samuel in the field shouting, "We have a new little housekeeper, Samuel!" and without waiting for a reply drives on to the house, to tell Annie and Jacob the news of the birth of their first grandchild.

There will be no special fuss made over this tiny new addition to the Amish community, no ceremonies, no pink blankets, no silver cup or spoon. But there is great joy in her arrival: the new parents, whose status is advanced another notch by the birth of their first child, consider the baby a gift from God, and they accept willingly the heavy responsibilities of nurturing and training this and each additional child that God will send them.

Amish life is based on large families who seem to enjoy their young children very much. Babies are immediately a part of the family, not isolated from it. Little Annie—they have decided to name the child after John's mother—will sleep in a crib in her parents' room when she is brought home from the hospital (most Amish babies today are born in hospitals). Her mother will change and bathe and dress her on her lap, and feed her on a schedule that suits the family's working routine. The baby will go with her mother to Sunday preaching, cuddled on her lap in the kitchen until she is old enough to be put to sleep with several other tiny children in one of the big upstairs beds. And she'll spend most of her waking hours in the company of her mother and father and other relatives.

When she's old enough to sit up and take some solid food, little Annie will join her family at the table, and they will share their meal with her. Eating together is important to the Amish, and Amish parents believe their children will be healthier and stronger if they eat with the family.

Leah Beiler is used to babies. She grew up in a big family, and as a teen-ager she helped take care of the four additional brothers and sisters who were born after she was twelve. Now Leah's mother is pregnant again, and as often happens in Amish families, her next child will be younger than her granddaughter. Leah was prepared for motherhood just as she was for marriage and the responsibilities of managing a household and helping her husband in the fields and taking her turn at having the Sunday preaching.

Leah is not worried about spoiling her baby with too much attention. The Amish feel that cranky, crying babies are made that way by nervous adults who are not comfortable around children. Although Leah and her family are generally relaxed, Leah is likely to become tense and protective about her child in the presence of outsiders. She does not want worldly people to make a special point of noticing her baby.

From the time of birth, Amish children are prepared for their roles in the family and in the Amish community. Sex typing begins immediately: girls are welcomed as "little housekeepers" and "dishwashers," boys are "little woodchoppers" and "farmers." Amish parents understand that their most important responsibility is the upbringing of the children. John and Leah will discover as Annie grows up and more children are born that the responsibility of being good models for their children affects their own behavior: John must be a diligent farmer in order to impress upon his sons the way in which they must work. Leah will be conscious of her habits as a housewife as she teaches her daughters what is expected of them.

From early on, John and Leah must agree on the way they will handle inevitable discipline problems; as parents they must speak and act as one. John remembers his own childhood, as the eldest in the family. His mother and father are of very different temperaments, and he knows how hard it must have been for them to act in accord. John had felt the switch on his behind frequently in his childhood, but he believes his brother Samuel, a rebellious child, must have set some kind of record for "smackings." Amish parents are rather liberal with the use of the switch, but it is said that they do not use it harshly.

John Beiler, gazing with pleasure at his sleeping daughter and thinking ahead to the time when he and Leah will be blessed with more sons and daughters, hopes mightily that he will have the wisdom to bring them up the right way.

Amos and Elam, awakened by the rumble and clash of thunder, dig deeper into their beds to block out the scary sound that rattles the windows and seems to be as close as the barnyard. Soon the storm passes over, and they sleep again until morning. They are at breakfast with the family when a neighbor comes by with the news: Solomon King's barn has been struck by lightning and burned to the ground.

Solomon's friends and neighbors and members of his church rally around to help him. For although Solomon carries no insurance (that would be a "yoke with the unbeliever"), the Amish take care of each other, in terms of both cash and physical labor, in time of disaster. Arrangements are made to lend horses and equipment to Solomon as he needs them. And the men begin planning for the barn raising—the *Scheierufschlagge*—to be held as soon as the materials can be rounded up. Money for materials comes from a fund maintained by the church and supplemented by additional donations.

Several days ahead of time a team of Amish carpenters begins cutting the timber to the correct dimensions of the new barn—Solomon has designed a bigger one than he had before—so that the work of the dozens of men who gather for the *Scheierufschlagge* is a matter of fitting the pieces together. Other advance work was also done by small groups, donating their time and energy: digging the enlarged foundation, preparing concrete in a gasoline-operated mixer, pouring the footings.

On the day of the barn raising, Jacob and Samuel, accompanied by the excited Amos and Elam who have announced that they too are big enough to help, start off early in the morning, as soon as the chores are finished. By seven o'clock a large contingent of men from all over the district has gathered in Solomon's barnyard, and with their combined muscle power the huge timbers are hauled into place. The young men, and some of the older ones, take this as an opportunity to show off their skill and fearlessness, stepping as easily among the high roof beams as city steelworkers. This is also an occasion for fun and horseplay—someone's hat is always nailed down, it seems —and lots of anecdotes of mashed thumbs and other boners are stored up for future repetition.

"Remember the barn raising at Adam Fisher's?" someone asks. They all do. That was the time Adam's son Ben fell and landed on a saw blade, cutting his leg right through to the bone. Fortunately, old Ruth Lapp was there, and she powwowed for Ben and stopped the bleeding then and there. Ben, who like a good many young Amish had little respect for *Brauche,* or powwowing as the "English" call sympathy-healing, was so impressed that he asked Ruth to pass the skill on to him. Traditionally, one can learn powwowing only from a person of the opposite sex to whom one promises secrecy of the Bible verses that are repeated silently as an incantation to effect the cure. Many Amish believe that powwowing can stop pain and bleeding and cure certain diseases. Others reject it or even condemn it as witchcraft. But for every handful of doubters there seems to be someone who knows a success story like Ben's. Most Amish prefer to be treated by medical doctors, although many fall prey to non-professional healers of various kinds.

Work on the new barn progresses quickly. Amos and Elam and other boys who have come to enjoy the sight of their fathers and brothers in this great cooperative venture are sent on errands, feeling fortunate that they have not been required to stay at home and help their mothers and sisters prepare the food that will be brought to Solomon's farm for the noon dinner.

The meal brings a respite and gives the men a chance for joking and conversation. Although the community project has a serious purpose, the men regard it as a holiday from regular farm work. The meal is, as usual, lavish. Afterwards, the women pack up the empty containers and leave, and the men resume their work. Throughout the afternoon the air is filled with the sounds of clattering hammers and scraping saws. By late afternoon, when the men must get home to the chores, the framework is complete and most of the sheathing is on. The carpenter who prefabricated the frame and a few helpers will return to take care of the finishing, but Solomon King now has a fine new barn.

While they were eating, Samuel's friends begin to brag

about their skill at corner ball, the most popular game among the Amish. The following Sunday is an off Sunday, and Samuel's friend Ike Lapp suggests, with a wink, that if Samuel can catch up on his sleep and get his strength back after whatever it is he has planned for Saturday night, they can come to his farm for a game.

Samuel ignores the jibe and agrees to the game. He has always been much better at corner ball than he has at baseball; wrestling, another favorite sport among the Amish, is not his idea of fun at all. Amos and Elam have told all their friends what a wonderful corner ball player their brother Samuel is, and they will be there, with choice seats on the fence rail, to lead the cheering for their favorite team.

Before the game, Ike will rake the barnyard level and cover it with a layer of clean straw. There are eight men on each team; the action is similar to dodge ball. Four men stand at the corners, and two men of the opposing team stand inside the square. The idea is to hit the men in the square with a soft ball. The young men in the middle demonstrate their agility by leaping and ducking to avoid the ball, and their opponents by passing the ball around fast and then firing it unexpectedly at one of the boys in the middle. The games sometimes go on for hours and attract crowds of highly partisan and exuberantly vocal spectators.

Jacob, meanwhile, is interested to hear his friends discussing the public auction to be held the following week at an "English" farm. Jacob knows that Annie will want to go. There might be some useful items at the sale. She has been saying that she would like to have some new pots and pans, and that Hannah will be needing a lot of plates and dishes and glassware when it is her turn to have Sunday preaching. There might be something John and Leah want for the new baby. Jacob tells Annie the news when he gets home for supper, but she has already heard it from the other women at the barn raising when she brought part of the dinner. It is arranged that they will combine a trip to the auction with some other errands in New Holland.

But their plans must be cancelled when Annie's sister brings the sad news that their father has died. The rest of the community will quickly be informed of the death of Daniel Lapp, and preparations for the funeral begin immediately. As in any time of trouble, friends and neighbors come to the assistance of the family. Annie and her brothers and sisters and her widowed mother are relieved of all responsibility for the funeral arrangements. No flowers are sent, but individual services are offered.

First old Daniel's coffin must be ordered. Daniel's long-time friend and neighbor, Amos Lapp, who is not directly related to him, takes the measurements of the body to the Amish carpenter who will construct the coffin to these specifications, using pine now that walnut has become scarce. The classic coffin shape, wider at the middle than at the ends, has a two-part lid, the upper part hinged so that Daniel can be viewed by the mourners for a last farewell. It is a plain box, without handles or lining. The style of the coffin is dictated by the *Ordnung;* in some groups the lid is one piece and is slid back a couple of feet for the viewing, and some groups also permit a lining of white cloth in the coffin.

If they had their choice, the Amish would not have the body embalmed. But the law requires embalming if the body is not buried within twenty-four hours of the death. Since some of Daniel's relatives will be coming from Kishacoquillas Valley and a few from Maryland, it is decided to hold the funeral on the third day. The local undertaker embalms the body and dresses it in white trousers, shirt, and socks, the "white raiment" specified by Scripture. When a woman dies, she is buried in the white shawl and apron which she has probably saved since her wedding day for this last occasion of her stay on earth.

Meanwhile, so that the family can stay with their elderly mother and receive the visitors who come to pay their respects, four young men of the neighborhood take over the farm work for the son with whom old Daniel lived, and another couple assumes responsibilities for the household chores.

Annie and the other brothers and sisters and their wives and husbands gather in the living room of the house, and the coffin containing Daniel's remains is moved into the living room.

On the day of the funeral the mourners gather silently. There is no conversation in the barnyard; instead, the mourners go directly into the house, where benches have been set up, as for a Sunday preaching. Following an introductory sermon, a preacher invited by Daniel's widow delivers a long sermon with many Biblical references, mostly from the Old Testament, strongly reminding the listeners of the necessity for leading a good life on earth in preparation for Eternal Life and a reunion in Heaven with the departed one. After the service ends, the room is rearranged so that the mourners can view Daniel's peaceful face for the last time, the men filing past the coffin first, followed by the women, while members of the family stand by and the minister reads a hymn. There is no singing at an Amish funeral.

Four pallbearers, chosen by Daniel's widow, set the coffin on a horse-drawn hearse, and another of Daniel's friends drives it slowly to the graveyard. The mourners follow behind in their buggies. The pallbearers dug the grave the day before, and the coffin, shut now with wooden screws, is lowered into a bottomless wooden vault to rest directly on the earth. More boards are placed on top, and the pallbearers begin to shovel earth onto the grave. The men, by custom, stand with their hats held on one side of their heads. When the grave is filled and the earth mounded over it, the family members get into their buggies and begin the slow drive back to Daniel's old home, followed by their friends and relatives. The mourners are served a sober but ample meal and support the grieving family with their comforting presence. The Amish feel that a meal helps everyone get on with the business of living.

Daniel Lapp has been "called home," but it is understood that his influence as head of the family will continue to make itself felt just as it did when he was alive, and just as his father, and his father's father before him, and all the persecuted ancestors who are part of the continuing tradition, laid their inescapable influence on Daniel's own life.

Reminders of "the world" surround the Amish on every side. MICHAEL RAMSEY

Author's Note

Kishacoquillas Valley, known locally as "Big Valley" (with the accent on *Big*), stretches between Jacks and Stone Mountains in central Pennsylvania and is the home of a large number of Amish. I grew up in Lewistown, a small town nearby, where the Amish came by horse and buggy to do their shopping, to visit the doctor, and to sell their produce at the farmer's market.

As a child I stared at them in their quaint costumes, confusing them with nuns from the local convent. Not all of the things I learned about them turned out to be true.

My grandparents, who had been farmers themselves, told me the Amish were excellent farmers, perhaps the best in the area, who had a lot of money and hid it on their farms. I knew that they didn't have electricity on those farms and that they weren't supposed to drive cars, which made it very confusing when I sometimes spotted a bearded Amish father behind the wheel of a black Chrysler with the chrome trim painted to match. (I know now they were Beachy Amish.)

It was said, but I never really believed, that they rarely took baths, sewing on their long underwear in the fall and not taking it off again until spring. We told "outsiders"—visitors who knew even less about the Amish— that they painted their gates blue to show that they had marriageable daughters, but we never once saw a blue gate in all our Sunday afternoon drives through Big Valley. The blue gate turned out to be a myth.

Nearly every year during the forties and early fifties we read in the local paper about Amish fathers who were jailed because they refused to send their children to school beyond the eighth grade. We thought they were being stubborn, but as stubborn "Pennsylvania Dutchmen" ourselves, we rather admired them without understanding their motives.

We had a unique folk society in our midst, but it had been there for so long that no one paid any attention to it, except for a few scholars at Pennsylvania State University on the other side of Big Valley.

Eventually I left Lewistown, returning only for occasional visits. Not long ago on one of those visits I stood outside the gates of the sprawling, dirty, noisy steel mill that was for years the economic backbone of the town as well as its principal source of air pollution. The mill cuts

*Children are bundled up against the cold
in Big Valley, Pennsylvania.* MICHAEL RAMSEY

an unsightly swath between the town, where turn-of-the-century frame houses crowd up against the sidewalks, and the beautiful hills and valleys with their well-kept farms. A horse and buggy, on its way from the valley to the town, rattled slowly past the mill, hugging in close to the chain-link fence. Traffic steered around them. A bearded young man in a black suit and a broad-brimmed hat held the reins. His wife wore a long purple dress, a black bonnet, and a black shawl, and the child on her lap was dressed exactly like her. On impulse—I had never done it before—I waved. The young man raised his hand; his wife smiled. The horse trotted briskly. And I knew that I wanted to learn about the Amish.

But the Amish are suspicious of outsiders, reluctant to talk to someone who wants to learn about them for the purpose of writing a book. Most books about the Amish have been written by non-Amish and the facts presented are frequently contradictory. But I found two excellent sources. John A. Hostetler, author of *Amish Society* and *Children in Amish Society,* was born in Big Valley and grew up in an Amish family. However, he went to college in defiance of Amish tradition, receiving his Ph.D. at Pennsylvania State University, and is now a university professor of anthropology and sociology. In the 1940s another Amish teacher and writer, Joseph W. Yoder, also from Big Valley, published the semi-fictionalized story of his family, *Rosanna of the Amish.* Although some non-Amish writers have lived for years among the Amish and gained a degree of acceptance from them, Hostetler and

Yoder are the best sources for sorting facts and dispelling myths.

In addition to reading, I spent time in Lancaster County, watching and asking questions. And I was invited to spend an evening at an Amish farm, after promising my intermediary, a Mennonite friend, not to announce myself as a writer and not to ask a lot of "nosey" questions.

I did my best not to play inquisitor, but the scene in the kitchen made me itch for a camera, or barring that, an indelible memory: the gray-bearded father, a man in his sixties, sat at the kitchen table working on his account book. Sharing the yellow light of the gas lamp was his wife, braiding a long rope of rye straw for a hat. The daughters of the house, middle-aged spinsters, had a quilting frame set up in the living room, and they asked me to join them. I had never quilted, and my large, clumsy stitches embarrassed me. "You can pull them out as soon as I've gone," I told them. They laughed, and we were at ease with each other. It was a pleasant evening, but although I did not learn facts about Amish culture, I did experience the warm feeling of a friendly Amish family.

There were visits with other families, always pleasant, but most of what I come to know about the Amish I learned from the few authoritative books I could find, from magazine and newspaper articles, and from asking questions of sympathetic and well-informed non-Amish people. I heard stories about buggy racing that got the young men into trouble with local authorities and about

Sheep are spectators to a lively ball game. MICHAEL RAMSEY

general hell-raising among the young that distresses both
Amish and non-Amish. I read reports of genetic defects,
such as dwarfism and polydactylism (having more than ten
fingers or toes) that plague the Amish, the result of intermarriage.

But eventually I began to have some comprehension of
the great complexity of the "simple life" of the unsophis-
ticated Amish. As I learned more and understood more, I
grew in my appreciation of this group of people who continue to flourish despite the dire predictions of writers of
a generation ago who thought they foresaw the disintegra-
tion of Amish society by the 1960s.

It is not my place to make predictions. I merely pass
on what I have learned with the fervent hope that the
Amish culture which has survived the persecutions of the
Middle Ages and the impact of modern technology will
endure. Let it be a reminder of the values that helped to
build America and that still have validity for all of us
who struggle to discern our goals and determine our di-
rections in an age that offers few touchstones.